T0064255

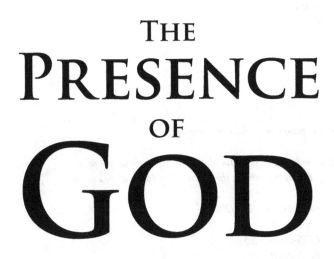

THE PRESENCE OF GOD

BETTY INGRAM GREEN

authorHOUSE®

AuthorHouse™
1663 Liberty Drive
Bloomington, IN 47403
www.authorhouse.com
Phone: 833-262-8899

Published by AuthorHouse 03/19/2021

ISBN: 978-1-6655-2055-3 (sc)
ISBN: 978-1-6655-2059-1 (e)

Library of Congress Control Number: 2021906077

Print information available on the last page.

Any people depicted in stock imagery provided by Getty Images are models, and such images are being used for illustrative purposes only. Certain stock imagery © Getty Images.

This book is printed on acid-free paper.

Scriptures quoted from King James Version, Public Domain

To my husband, Rev. Tommie Green; my son, Marion County Deputy Sheriff Sgt. Terrence Green; and my grandson, Terrence II.

To my physical family, Pastor James Harlan, Lonnie, Johnny, Faye, and Shirley, and my spiritual family!

CONTENTS

OUR HEARTS ACHE

Our hearts ache being reminded daily of the coronavirus pandemic that attacked America and the world, introducing itself to us in the early months of 2020.

Our hearts ache because of the 237,584-plus deaths across America, the 1,257,922-plus deaths globally, and the fear, anxiety, and frustration the virus is causing.

Our hearts ache!

Our hearts ache because in the midst of this pandemic, in our beloved America, once again, racism, a deep, dark, infected wound embedded in the hearts of some, had the nerves to stick its ugly head up again.

Our hearts ache!

Our hearts ache severely for yet another African American male, a native of Minneapolis, and several other Black males across this great country of ours who have lost their lives due to hatred, lack of love, and lack of concern for their fellow man.

Our hearts ache!

Our hearts ache when protesters exercising their First Amendment rights at times found themselves in the presence of riots, tear gas, rubber bullets, arrests, hatred, and threats.

Our hearts ache!

Our hearts ache remembering the pain African American families suffered because of the loss of loved ones at the hands of several law enforcement officers sworn to serve and protect.

Our hearts ache!

Our hearts ache because of several police officers' lack of compassion for human life when yet another Black man was crying, "I can't breathe!" while a knee was applied to his neck.

Our hearts ache!

Our hearts ache at the outpouring of witnesses and innocent bystanders' cries for mercy for human life, but no compassion or mercy was found.

Our hearts ache!

Our hearts ache when injustice of any kind takes place in our beloved America and the entire world sits watching our struggle with compassion, making it complicated to hold down our young people and especially our Generation X and millennials.

Our hearts ache!

My heart aches for the hard-working, faithful, and dedicated men and women of our law enforcement departments who are putting their lives on the line every day, though some have been falsely accused, and for officers' families that have suffered great loss as well.

My heart aches!

My heart was warmed, and I developed teary eyes witnessing Black and White Americans and people of other cultures walking together arm in arm, hand in hand, peacefully for a common cause, for the good of humankind crying, "Black lives matter!" and "Enough is enough!"

My heart rejoices!

My heart is greatly moved when other nationalities of the world feel African Americans' pain, stand, and organize protests in their countries, crying, "Black lives matter!"

My heart rejoices!

My heart leaps for joy as I develop a sense of pride when members of our law enforcement department in Indiana embrace protesters, walk a block with them, and listen to their cries outside our governor's mansion.

My heart is merry!

My heart is overjoyed knowing Jesus can calm the raging storm and still the wind and waves in our hearts when we cry out, "Lord, I cannot take much more!"

I ask the Lord to stand by me, walk with me, hold my hand, and carry if need be my family, my friends, and me. His presence massages all aching hearts.

CHAPTER 1

⚜

TRAIN UP A CHILD

In times like these, we need a friend. In times like these, we need a Savior. In times like these, we need Jesus. In times like these, our children, our precious gifts from God, must have solid foundations—something or someone they can trust.

When my son, Terrence, was about four, my husband, Tommie, and I would read and teach Bible stories to him. As he grew older, we bought Christian tapes, and our son would listen to Bible stories each night before he fell asleep. Never did we force Bible stories on him. He would ask for a Bible character or story each night while clinging to his teddy bear.

Some of his favorite Bible characters and stories were Joseph and his brothers, Moses, Noah, Daniel in the lions' den, Jonah, David and Goliath, and Samson and his parents especially, Samson's father, Manoah. He was trouble with the fall of Samson by trusting Delilah and the action of Samson's enemies, the Philistines.

My son's favorite hero in the Bible was and still is Jesus.

My husband and I went a step further; we enrolled him in a Christian daycare, Noah's Ark, so he learned scriptures at school as well as at home.

Jesus loved children!

> Then were there brought unto him little children, that he should put his hands on them, and pray: and the disciples rebuked them. But Jesus said, suffer (permit) little children, and forbid them not, to come unto me: for

of such is the kingdom of heaven. And he laid his hands
on them, and departed thence. (Matthew 19:13–15)

Equipping our children in the knowledge, love, and reverence for God
is a key factor to a fulfilling life in Christ. We can do nothing without God.

Train up a child in the way he should go: and when he is
old, he will not depart from it. (Proverbs 22:6)

We all remember this scripture, but do we heed it? Godly training
is commanded for our children. What God-fearing parents want their
children (precious gifts from God) to forget or neglect their godly training,
faithfulness, beliefs, culture, and moral values? The right answer should
be no parent. Am I right?

Children, obey your parents in the Lord: for this is
right. Honour thy father and mother; (which is the first
commandment with promise) That it may be well with
thee, and thou mayest live long on the earth.

That is the one of the main points we want to drive home to our
children today. We must deliver obedience to parents and love for God to
our young ones.

Our children have a responsibility to God as well. God smiles on
obedience from children.

And, ye fathers, provoke not your children to wrath: but
bring them up in the nurture and admonition of the Lord.
(Ephesians 6:1–4)

In 1 Samuel, we read, "It is better to obey the Lord than to sacrifice."
The temptations or tests of life cause many of us to sometime leave
temporary those things we know that are right, and even good for us, go
astray, and fall short of the glory of God.

For ALL have sinned, and come short of the glory of God.
(Romans 3:23)

That all means everyone. I believe Jesus stated it best when he said, "He that is without sin, let him cast the first stone." Some of us are so self-righteous that Jesus wrote in the dirt (the Pharisees), when addressing the adulterous woman's sin.

What then is sin?

Sin is the transgression of the law.

Whose law?

God's law.

Then who is exempt?

If sin can tip up on adults, what about our children?

We have all been taught that when we fall down, we don't have to stay down. Our presenting Jesus to our children at an early age will help prepare them to get up and start anew when they do fall down.

We believers in Christ must die daily to the flesh, pray always that our lives be controlled by the aid of the Holy Spirit, the presence of God, and seize the opportunity to teach these things to our children as best we can and according to their understanding.

Shall we continue in sin? God forbid! There are consequences to sin, but remember that Jesus paid the price for sin by dying and rising. All parents want the best for our children. We want our children to have as smooth a journey as possible throughout life and make the necessary investments for the next life with Christ.

There will be bumps in the road, but remember—Jesus can make the crooked roads straight!

CHAPTER 2

⁓

JOB, A RIGHTEOUS MAN, WEATHERS THE STORM

Job was a righteous man who encountered several tremendous storms in his life. Did he give up when he ran into curves in the road? No. He kept the faith in the midst of his suffering.

Job is known for the following popular scriptures including, "Though he slay me, yet will I trust in him: But I will maintain mine own ways before him." Job was saying to God, "Even if you kill me, I will still trust that you know best, Lord, and I will maintain my innocence. I am not guilty of any sin." Job, a man known for patience, longed for vindication.

He is known for other popular statements as well.

> Man that is born of a woman is of a few days, and full of trouble. (Job 14:1)

> If a man dies, shall he live again? All the days of my appointed time will I wait, till my change come. (Job 14:14)

Job longed for death; he felt it would be a relief from his troubles and suffering. Did Job sin?

Have you ever thought, perhaps God wants to brag on us sometimes? Or perhaps bring us into complete trust in him wiping away our self-righteousness and pride? Maybe, at times, we just plainly think too highly of ourselves. Just maybe, perhaps, God is trying to grab our attention and tell us something.

Is it possible to know the mind of God? Have you ever asked God, "Lord, why so much pain?"? Remember, it rains on the just as well as the unjust.

Let's walk with Job for a few minutes and watch the handiwork of God.

> Job, a perfect and upright man. A man that feared God,
> and eschewed evil. (Job 1:1)

Job was a rich man with moral and spiritual qualities. He shunned evil, but some would say, he fell short of God's standard of perfection. No, Job was not sinless. He said, "Man that is born of a woman is of a few days, and full of trouble" (Job 14:1).

Job's enemy as well as our enemy was Satan, but keep in mind, Satan only has the power God allows him to have.

Thus far, can I trust we are on the same page?

> Now, there was a day when the sons of God came to
> present themselves before the Lord, and Satan came also
> among them.

The sons of God are heavenly beings, angels. Remember, Satan is an angelic being.

> And the Lord said unto Satan, Whence comest thou?
> Then Satan answered the Lord, and said, From going to
> and fro in the earth, and from walking up and down in it.

Satan has access to the earth and the freedom to move around on it. Satan will continue to move about the earth until he is bound for the thousand years during the millennium; after that, he will be cast into the lake of fire forever. That is Satan's future! Remind Satan of his destination sometimes, and he will surely flee.

Is Satan busy going to and fro in the earth and walking up and down in it?

Permission from God

> And the Lord said unto Satan, Hast thou considered
> my servant Job, that there is none like him in the earth,
> a perfect and upright man, one that feareth God, and
> escheweth evil?

Job had found favor with God. It is good for us sometimes to just look at the person in the mirror, examine ourselves, and ask ourselves, *Am I in God's favor? Or am I a stumbling-block for other Christians on this faith journey?*

> Then Satan answered the Lord, and said, Doth Job fear
> God for nought?

Satan was saying to God in essence, "Job is serving you, God, because you are taking care of him in every way. God, you got Job covered!"

> Hast not thou made an hedge about him, and about his
> house, and about all that he hath on every side? thou
> has blessed the work of his hands, and his substance is
> increased in the land. But, put forth thine hand now, and
> touch all that he hath, and he will curse thee to thy face.

What nerve! Satan talking to and charging God in this way!

Permission Given by God to Trouble Job

> And the Lord said unto Satan, Behold, all that he has is
> in thy power, only upon himself put not forth thine hand.
> So, Satan went forth from the presence of the Lord.

Satan attacked Job's possessions, animals, and servants, and he killed Job's children.

> Job tore his robe, shaved his head, fell to the ground, and
> worshipped the Lord.

Job passed the test, and he said, "Naked came I out of my mother's womb, and naked shall I return thither: the Lord gave, and the Lord hath taken away: blessed be the name of the Lord. In all this Job sinned not, nor charged God foolishly" (Job 1:6–12, 18–22).

Satan does not give up. He may go away for a while, but I can guarantee you, he will return.

> Again there was a day when the sons of God came to present themselves before the Lord, and Satan came also among them to present himself before the Lord. And the Lord said unto Satan, from whence comest thou? And Satan answered the Lord, and said, From going to and fro in the earth, and from walking up and down in it.

> And the Lord said unto Satan, Hast thou considered my servant Job, that there is none like him in the earth, a perfect and upright man, one that feareth God, and escheweth evil? and still he holdeth fast his integrity, although thou movedst me against him, to destroy him without cause.

Have you ever wondered trials, temptations, and suffering are present in the lives of believers? Are we supposed to live carefree lives in this dispensation of grace? Just maybe, perhaps, God is allowing some of these mishaps for our own good. You think?

God does not tempt us to do evil.

> And Satan answered the Lord, and said, Skin for skin, yea, all that a man hath will he give for his life. But put forth thine hand now and touch his bone and his flesh, and he will curse thee to thy face.

> And the Lord said unto Satan, behold, he is in thine hand; but save his life.

Do you believe you would have passed the test?

> So went Satan forth from the Presence of the Lord, and smote Job with sore boils from the sole of his foot unto his crown. And he took him a potsherd (broken pottery) to scrape himself withal; and he sat down among the ashes.

Job's skin itched constantly. He was in severe pain. His flesh attracted worms; it oozed, grew crusty, and turned dark. Job experienced fever and aching bones.

What suffering? Job's wife!

> Then said Job's wife unto him, Dost thou still retain thine integrity? Curse God, and die.

Sometimes, those closest to us can give us bad advice. Job's wife was grief-stricken over the loss of her children, and she was also very angry. She concluded that Job was suffering because God was unfair. Have you ever felt this way about God in your times of trouble? We have all had our share of troubles.

> But he said unto her, Thou speakest as one of the foolish women speaketh. What? shall we receive good at the hand of God, and shall we not receive evil? In all this did not Job sin with his lips. (Job 2:1–10)

Job's friends Eliphaz, Bildad, and Zophar accused him of having sinned against God as well. Job did curse the day he was born, and he became a critic of God.

> Then the Lord answered Job out of the whirlwind, and said, who is this that darkeneth counsel by words without knowledge? Gird up now thy loins like a man; for I will demand of thee, and answer thou me. Where wast thou when I laid the foundation of the earth? Declare, if thou has understanding. (Job 38:1–4)

The Lord was asking Job, "Where were you, Job when I created the stars, the universe, the earth, and the angels? In other words, where were you when I created creation? Did I require your input Job then? Now, Job, what makes you think I need your help now?" We do not have the understanding, knowledge, and wisdom of God, our Creator. He does not need our help.

God knows what's best for us even though at times we tend to believe we are better at handling our affairs and especially during those times when God seems to be quiet, move slowly, or does not move when we want him to move. Do you agree?

Job repented to the Lord.

> Then Job answered the Lord, and said, I know that thou canst do every thing, and that no thought can be withholden from thee. Who is he that hideth counsel without knowledge? Therefore have I uttered that I understood not; things too wonderful for me, which I knew not. Hear, I beseech thee, and I will speak: I will demand of thee, and declare thou unto me. I have heard of thee by the hearing of the ear: but now mine eye seeth thee. Wherefore I abhor myself, and repent in dust and ashes.

Job repented of pride and rebellion. He humbled himself and praised God. He found contentment in God's fellowship.

If we know God, do we need to know why we go through such trials and tribulations? Yet we find ourselves asking God, "Why, Lord? Why so much pain? Lord, this storm is too much for me! Remember, you said you would not put no more on me than I could bear."

God loves us, and he is still in control of our lives just as he was in control of Job's life. God is still in control of the whole universe.

And the Lord turned the captivity of Job, when he prayed for his friends; also, the Lord gave Job twice as much as he had before.

9

Family Support

Job's family came and brought love, money, and gold to him.

> So, the Lord blessed the latter end of Job's life more than his beginning: for he had fourteen thousand sheep, and six thousand camels, and a thousand yoke of oxen, and a thousand she asses. He had also seven sons and three daughters. Job lived an hundred and forty years, and saw his sons, and his sons' sons, even four generations. (Job 42:1–6, 10–12, 16)

Remember, Satan was allowed to go only so far; God was in the midst of Job's storm. Satan was an enemy of Job, and he is also our enemy, right? Satan has only the power God allows him to have. Satan is already defeated. Sometimes, that statement can be hard to believe, but it is so true.

We have to trust, believe, and abide in the Word of God for insight and wisdom just as Job had to. We must never credit our own understanding that we know the mind of God.

Do not you recall the statement, "If the Lord be willing"?

Satan wants to overthrow God and run his evil course, but his arms are still too short to box with God as the saying goes. Satan desires to have us, to make merchandise of us, to shame us, and cause us to disobey God. He works at deceit and lies. Remember, he was a liar from the beginning.

Let's revisit the Garden of Eden in the next chapter. Keep reading!

CHAPTER 3

✍

IN THE BEGINNING

In the beginning was the word, and the word was with God, and the word was God. The same was in the beginning with God. (John 1:1–2)
Even before time began, Christ was in existence with God.

> All things were made by him: and without him was not any thing made that was made. In him was life; and the life was the light of men. (John 1:3–4)

Man's job is to manage the earth, to protect and preserve it.

> And God said, Let us make man in our image, after our likeness: and let them have dominion over the fish of the sea, and over the fowl of the air, and over the cattle, and over all the earth, and over every creeping thing that creepeth upon the earth.

Notice the statement "Let us make man in our image." Who was the "us" and "our" in these verses? The Trinity—Father, Son, and Holy Spirit. All three persons of the Godhead were involved in creation.

You know the story: "And the Lord God formed man of the dust of the ground, and breathed into his nostrils the breath of life, and man became a living soul." Amen!

God's Great Command

> And the Lord God commanded the man, saying, of every tree of the garden thou mayest freely eat: But of the tree of the knowledge of good and evil, thou shall not eat of it: for in the day that thou eatest thereof thou shalt surely die.

It's not good for man to be alone.

> And the Lord said, it is not good that the man should be alone: I will make him an help meet for him.

Man and woman together.

> And the Lord God caused a deep sleep to fall upon Adam, and he slept: and he took one of his ribs, and closed up the flesh instead thereof.

Woman Created—Marriage Instituted

> And the rib which the Lord God had taken from man, made he a woman and brought her unto the man. And Adam said, This is now bone of my bones, and flesh of my flesh: she shall be called woman, because she was taken out of man.

If a man loves himself and will not harm himself, does the same principle apply to his wife?

> Therefore shall a man leave his father and his mother, and shall cleave unto his wife: and they shall be one flesh.

There is no room for a threesome here. Are we on the same page? There are no ifs, ands, or buts about this scripture; the wife comes right after God in the husband's life.

And they were both naked, the man and his wife, and were not ashamed. (Genesis 1:26, 2:7, 16, 17, 21–25)

The Serpent

The serpent was more subtil (clever) than any beast of the field which the Lord had made. And he said unto the woman, Yea, hath God said, Ye shall not eat of every tree of the garden?

We must listen closely to who is speaking to us today. Is it the voice of God or the voice of Satan? To know the voice of God, we have to know his Word. We are to always line up spoken statements with the holy scriptures.

And the woman said unto the serpent, We may eat of the fruit of the trees of the garden: But of the fruit of the tree which is in the midst of the garden, God hath said, Ye shall not eat of it, neither shall ye touch it, lest ye die.

Satan's Big Lie

And the serpent said unto the woman, "Ye shall not surely die." (Genesis 3:1–4)

That old sly devil! He never changes his strategy or his crafty ways. The same tricks he used on our forefathers he still attempts to use on us.

Satan does not work alone. He has many helpers out there. Remember, Jesus's words to the Jews.

You are of your father the devil, and the lusts of your father ye will do. He was a murderer from the beginning, and abode not in the truth, because there is no truth in him. When he speaketh a lie, he speaketh of his own: for he is a liar, and the father of it. (John 8:44)

Do you believe the real or true reason for not accepting Christ as Savior for many unbelievers is their relationship with the devil or love of worldly things?

Do Not Add to God's Word

Take notice of the two incidents that happened with Eve. First, she added to what God had said to her and Adam by stating that they were not even to touch the tree. Second, Satan lied and said they would not surely die. Eve ate the forbidden fruit and gave it to Adam, who ate some as well. This act of disobedience caused a spiritual separation from God. Yes, they died spiritually.

Later, the two would die physically. Their disobedience caused total chaos, a change that would affect them and generations to come. Adam's and Eve's sense of awareness was opened; they came to the conclusion that they were naked, and they became ashamed.

> Lust had been conceived and brought forth sin, and sin
> when it was finished brought forth death. (James 1:15)

Their sin even affected nature and the animal kingdom. We have all watched *Wild Kingdom* and other documentaries exhibiting wild animals devouring each other. The lion and the sheep no longer could lie down together.

Adam and Eve had broken fellowship with God. They used leaves to cover themselves, and they attempted to hide from the presence of God.

Now, humankind needed a Savior. God already had a plan for Jesus to come and redeem humanity.

Satan's Mission

Satan tends to darken our light and hurt our testimony if we do not abide in the Word of God. Satan, his demons, and people who allow him to use them tend to cause us trouble, trials, and tribulation. Where there is peace, Satan works to cause war. Where there is trust, Satan works to cause distrust using anyone open to him.

Those believers in the household of faith stand guard. We tend to be Satan's main target. He wants our mouths closed when it comes to mentioning the name of Jesus.

Hasn't that always been the case? Even the early disciples and apostles were ordered not to preach or teach in the name of Jesus.

Satan even works at causing pain in our homes and hearts with our spouses, children, and grandchildren. Again, Satan hates peace, Christians of one accord, fellowshipping of the saints, and reading and sharing the gospel. He is the author of confusion, deceit, wickedness ... The list goes on ...

But God can make something good out of confusion because he is God. Nothing is too hard for him! Where there is division, frustration, and confusion, look around for Satan and his workers. If you do not already know this, wake up! We all must come to the conclusion that any enemy of God is our enemy as well.

Do Not Tempt God

Jesus was led up of the Holy Spirit into the wilderness to be tempted of the devil (Matthew 3:16–17, 4:1). So who are we when we are tempted by the devil? Jesus sinned not! Jesus used the Word to send Satan away.

> It is written, man shall not live by bread alone, but by every word that proceedeth out of the mouth of God. (Matthew 4:4)

> It is written again, thou shalt not tempt the Lord thy God. (Matthew 4:7)

> Get thee hence, Satan: For it is written, thou shalt worship the Lord thy God, and him only shalt thou serve. (Matthew 4:10)

For us Christians in this dispensation of grace, another sure way of sending Satan hence is to remind him of his destination—the lake of fire.

Satan uses tricks of frustration, division, and confusion in our lives to hinder us. He hates the presence of God and the Holy Spirit of God, which dwells in us Christians. He wants us to focus on everything and anything other than Jesus.

Satan is an enemy of Jesus and his heirs, and we Christians are Jesus's heirs; we have been adopted into the body of Christ.

CHAPTER 4

‹∾›

OLD TESTAMENT PATRIOTS SAID YES TO THE LORD

Abraham, the Father of Faith

We have Abraham, the father of faith and friend of God. Abraham was declared righteous and justified by faith long before the apostle Paul.

Leave Your Home, Abraham!

> Now the Lord had said unto Abram, Get thee out of thy country, from thy kindred, and from thy father's house, unto a land that I would shew thee. And I will make of thee a great nation, and I will bless thee, and make thy name great; and thy shalt be a blessing: And I will bless them that bless thee, and curse him that curseth thee: and in thee shall all families of the earth be blessed. Abraham took Sarai his wife, and Lot his brother's son, and all their substance that they had gathered, and the souls that they had gotten in Haran; and they went forth to go into the land of Canaan; and into the land of Canaan they came. (Genesis 12:1–5)

A strange land it was. Notice that Abraham took Lot, his nephew. Remember that God told Abraham to leave his kindred. Later, Abraham would suffer for this act of disobedience.

The Lord Visited Abraham

One day, Abraham had a special meal prepared for the Lord, and the two men who that was with him (angels), and they did eat. A close friend of Abraham, God informed Abraham that Sarah would bare him a son. The Lord also told Abraham of the great cry of Sodom and Gomorrah and their sin. The two men (angels) turned their faces from thence, and went toward Sodom: but Abraham stood yet before the Lord, the presence of God.

What a Friend

Abraham knew Lot was in Sodom and begged God not to destroy the righteous with the wicked.

Peradventure there be fifty righteous within the city: wilt thou also destroy and not spare the place for the fifty righteous that are therein? And the Lord said, If I find in Sodom fifty righteous within the city, then I will spare all the place for their sakes. And Abraham answered and said, Behold now, I have taken upon me to speak unto the Lord, which am but dust and ashes: Peradventure there shall lack five of the fifty righteous: wilt thou destroy all the city for lack of five? And he said, If I find there forty and five, I will not destroy it. And he spake unto him yet again, and said, peradventure there shall be forty found there. and he said, I will not do it for forty's sake. And he said unto him, Oh let not the Lord be angry, and I will speak: Peradventure there shall thirty be found there. And he said, I will not do it, if I find thirty there. And he said, Behold now, I have taken upon me to speak unto the Lord: Peradventure there shall be twenty found there. And he said, I will not destroy it for twenty's sake. And he said, Oh let not the Lord be angry, and I will speak yet but this once: Peradventure ten shall be found there. And he said, I will not destroy it for ten's sake. (Genesis 18:23–33)

Words cannot express how good, merciful, and long-suffering God is. He was merciful and agreed that if only ten righteous were found in Sodom, he would not destroy the city, but only four individuals were led out of that wicked city by the hands of the angels.

Then the Lord rained upon Sodom and upon Gomorrah brimstone and fire from the Lord out of heaven; And he overthrew those cities, and all the plain, and all the inhabitants of the cities, and that which grew upon the ground.

Lot's wife loved Sodom and Gomorrah. We know her heart was still in Sodom.

But his wife looked back from behind him, and she became a pillar of salt. (Genesis 19:24–26)

Later, Jesus used this event of Lot's wife looking back as a warning for others about looking back. The lesson is this: Give God your heart, and be prepared for the coming of Christ. Love not the world more than God!

Sins Named in Sodom and Gomorrah

In Romans 1:24–32, the apostle Paul wrote of some of the sins that were also found in Sodom and Gomorrah.

God gave them up to uncleanness, idolatry, animals worshippers, gang rape, vile affection, lack of hospitality, even the women did change the "natural use" into that which is against nature. Men were found that had left the "natural use" of the women.

Sodom and Gomorrah was destroyed by God.

Abraham—A Friend of God Continued

Abraham, a friend of God, enjoyed being in his presence. He loved God so much that he was willing to sacrifice his son of promise, Isaac, whom he had fathered in his old age. Abraham was a hundred when Isaac was born and was still willing to obey God.

Abraham's Offering and Obedience to God

> And it came to pass after these things, that God did tempt Abraham; and he said, behold, here am I. And he said, Take now thy son, Thine only son Isaac, whom thou lovest, and get thee into the land of Moriah; and offer him there for a burnt offering upon one of the mountains which I will tell thee of.

Thou only son whom thou lovest ... Do you see the connections? Later, God would send his only begotten son as a sacrifice for us.

> And Abraham rose up early in the morning, and saddled his ass, and took two of his young men with him, and Isaac his son, and clave the wood for the burnt offering, and rose up, and went unto the place of which God had told him. Then on the third day Abraham lifted up his eyes, and saw the place afar off. And Abraham said unto his young men, Abide ye here with the ass; and I and the lad will go younder and worship, and come again to you.

Abraham had enough faith to believe that he and Isaac would return. Abraham believed God and in the resurrection.

> And Abraham took the wood of the burnt offering, and laid it upon Isaac his son; and he took the fire in his hand, and a knife; and they went both of them together. And Isaac spake unto Abraham his father, and said, My father:

and he said, Here am I, my son. And he said, Behold
the fire and the wood: but where is the lamb for a burnt
offering?

Isaac trusted Abraham his father, and he also exercised obedience
knowing that Abraham was a friend of God.

God Will Provide

And Abraham said, My son, God will provide himself
a lamb for a burnt offering: so they went both of them
together. And they came to the place which God had told
him of; and Abraham built an altar there, and laid the
wood in order, and bound Isaac his son, and laid him on
the altar upon the wood.

What would you have done? We say we love God and wish to obey him.

And Abraham stretched forth his hand, and took the
knife to slay his son. And the angel of the Lord called unto
him out of heaven, and said, Abraham, Abraham: And he
said, Here am I. And he said, Lay not thine hand upon the
lad, neither do thou any thing unto him: For now I know
that thou fearest God, seeing thou hast not withheld thy
son, thine only son from me. (Genesis 22:1–12)

Abraham passed the test! God is not slack concerning his promises.
He had promised to bless Sarah and give Abraham a son, and he kept his
word even though Abraham and Sarah had laughed at the thought of
having a son.

Then Abraham fell upon his face, and laughed, and said
in his heart, Shall a child be born unto him that is an
hundred years old? and shall Sarah, that is ninty years old,
bear? (Genesis 17:16–17)

> Therefore Sarah laughed within herself, saying, After I am waxed old shall I have pleasure, my lord being old also? And the Lord said unto Abraham, Wherefore did Sarah laugh, saying, Shall I of a surety bear a child, which am old? Is anything too hard for the Lord? At the time appointed I will return unto thee, according to the time of life, and Sarah shall have a son. (Genesis 18:12–14)

> And the Lord visited Sarah as he had said, and the Lord did unto Sarah as he had spoken. For Sarah conceived, and bare Abraham a son in his old age, at the set time of which God had spoken to him. And Abraham called the name of his son that was born unto him, whom Sarah bare to him, Isaac. And Abraham was an hundred years old, when his son Isaac was born unto him. (Genesis 21:1–3, 5)

God had rejuvenated Abraham's and Sarah's bodies to bear a son and for Sarah to nurse him. Now that's something to shout and talk about!

Out of the lineage of Abraham, we were given Isaac, and his son, Jacob, the father of twelve sons who became known as the twelve tribes of Israel.

Moses—One Whom the Lord Knew Face to Face

Moses was asked to remove his shoes because he was on holy ground when he was in the presence of God.

> And the angel of the Lord appeared unto him in a flame of fire out of the midst of a bush: and he looked, and, behold, the bush burned with fire, and the bush was not consumed. And Moses said, I will now turn aside, and see this great sight why the bush is not burnt. And when the Lord saw that he turned aside to see, God called unto him out of the midst of the bush, and said, Moses Moses. And he said, Here am I.

Are you saying yes to the Lord today?

> And he said, Draw not nigh hither: put off thy shoes from
> off thy feet, for the place whereon thou standest is holy
> ground. Moreover he said, I am the God of thy father, the
> God of Abraham, the God of Isaac, and the God of Jacob.
> And Moses hid his face, for he was afraid to look upon
> God. And the Lord said, I have surely seen the affliction
> of my people which are in Egypt, and have heard their cry
> by reason of their taskmasters; for I know their sorrows.

God knows just how much we can bear. He might not come when we
want him to, but he is always on time.

Come, Lord Jesus, and Deliver Us

> And I am come down to deliver them out of the hand of
> the Egyptians, and to bring them up out of that land unto
> a good land and a large, unto a land flowing with milk
> and honey. (Exodus 3:2–8)

Did not Moses show reluctance in the beginning to what God was
asking him to do?

> And Moses said unto God, Who am I, that I should go
> unto Phar'aoh, and that I should bring forth the children
> of Israel out of Egypt. (Exodus 3:11)

> And Moses said unto the Lord, O my Lord, I am not
> eloquent, neither heretofore, nor since thou hast spoken
> unto thy servant: but I am slow of speech, and of a slow
> tongue.

Moses was saying, "Lord, I cannot talk right!"

And the Lord said unto him, Who hath made man's mouth? or who maketh the dumb, or deaf, or the seeing, or the blind? have not I the Lord? Now therefore go, and I will be with thy mouth, and teach thee what thou shalt say. And he said, O my Lord, send, I pray thee, by the hand of him whom thou wilt send.

How is your faith adding up today? Are you willing to trust and obey God? Are you saying yes or no to God today?

And the anger of the Lord was kindled against Moses, and he said, Is not Aaron the Levite thy brother? I know that he can speak well. And also, behold, he cometh forth to meet thee: and when he seeth thee, he will be glad in his heart. And thou shall speak unto him, and put words in his mouth: and I will be with thy mouth, and with his mouth, and will teach you what ye shall do (the presence of God). And he shall be thy spokesman unto the people: and he shall be, even he shall be to thee instead of a mouth, and thou shalt be to him instead of God. And thou shalt take this rod in thine hand, wherewith thou shalt do signs. (Exodus 4:10–17)

First Encounter with Pharaoh

And afterward Moses and Aaron went in, and told Pharaoh, Thus saith the Lord God of Israel, Let my people go, that they may hold a feast unto me in the wilderness. And Pharaoh said, Who is the Lord, that I should obey his voice to let Israel go? I know not the Lord, neither will I let Israel go. And the Lord said unto Moses, See, I have made thee A God to Pharaoh: and Aaron thy brother shall be thy prophet. Thou shall speak all that I command thee: and Aaron thou brother shall speak unto Pharaoh, that he send the children of Israel out of his land.

Second Encounter with Pharaoh

> And Moses and Aaron went in unto Pharaoh, and they did so as the Lord had commanded: and Aaron cast down his rod before Pharaoh and it became a Serpent. Then Pharaoh also called the wise men and the sorcerers; now the magicians of Egypt, they also did in like manner with their enchantments. For they cast down every man his rod, and they became serpents: but Aaron's rod swallowed up their rods.

Pharaoh's Heart Hardened by God

> And he hardened Pharaoh's heart, that he hearkened not unto them, as the Lord had said. (Exodus 5:1–2, 7:1–2, 10–13)

Several plagues were instituted upon Egypt because of the hardening of Pharaoh's heart; they came in the following forms: blood, frogs, lice, flies, disease on the beasts, boils on man and beast, hail, locusts, darkness, and the death of firstborn children.

The Passover

For the Passover, a lamb without blemish had to be killed and its blood put on the doorposts of God's people's homes.

> And the blood shall be to you for a token upon the houses where ye are: And when I see the blood, I will pass over you, and the plague shall not be upon you to destroy you, when I smite the land of Egypt. And this day shall be unto you for a memorial, and ye shall keep it a feast to the Lord throughout your generations: ye shall keep it a feast by an ordiance for ever. (Exodus 12:13–14)

An Illustration of Things to Come

Jesus, a lamb without blemish, a perfect sacrifice for us, paid the price on Calvary with his holy blood.

Let My People Go!

> And Pharaoh rose up in the night, he, and all his servants, and all the Egyptians; and there was a great cry in Egypt; and there was not a house where there was not one dead. And he called for Moses and Aaron by night, and said, Rise up, and get you forth from among my people, both ye and the children of Israel; and go, serve the Lord, as ye have said. Also take your flocks and your herds, as you have said, and be gone; and bless me also. (Exodus 12:30–32)

Pharaoh had lost his son as well. He had enough sense to ask Moses to bless him. He came to realize the power to release the children of Israel was not in his hands after all. Pharaoh concluded that the God of the Israelites was the one true God, a God Pharaoh's arms were too short to box with. Won't God make your enemies your footstool as well?

Exercising faith and obedience and staying in God's presence, Moses was able with the mighty hand of God and the help of Aaron to deliver the children of Israel from Egypt.

The Red Sea

The Lord was with Moses throughout the journey. God divided the Red Sea, and the children of Israel traveled on dry ground through the sea.

> And Moses stretched out his hand over the sea; and the Lord caused the sea to go back by a strong east wind all that night, and made the sea dry land, and the waters were divided. And the children of Israel went into the midst of the sea upon dry ground: and the waters were

a wall unto them on their right hand, and on their left. (Exodus 14:21–22)

The Promised Land

And the Lord said unto him, This is the land which I sware unto Abraham, unto Isaac, and unto Jacob, saying, I will give it unto thy seed: I have caused thee to see it with thine eyes, but thou shall not go over thither.

Moses went to the mountain top and saw the Promised Land, but God did not permit him to enter.

Do you remember the words of Dr. Martin Luther King Jr. about his having been to the mountain top, and seeing the Promised Land?

Death of Moses

So Moses the servant of the Lord died there in the land of Moab, according to the word of the Lord. And the children of Israel wept for Moses in the plains of Moab thirty days: so the days of weeping and mourning for Moses were ended. And there arose not a prophet since in Israel like unto Moses, whom the Lord knew face to face. In all the signs and the wonders, which the Lord sent him to do in the land of Egypt to Pharaoh, and to all his servants, and to all his land. And in all that mighty hand, and in all the great terror which Moses shewed in the sight of all Israel. (Deuteronomy 34:4–5, 8, 10–12)

Joshua—A New Leader and a Great Warrior

And Joshua the son of Nun was full of the spirit of wisdom; for Moses had laid his hands upon him: and the children of Israel hearkened unto him, and did as the Lord commanded Moses. (Deuteronomy 34:9)

Now after the death of Moses the servant of the Lord it came to pass, that the Lord spake unto Joshua, the son Nun, Moses' minister, saying, Moses my servant is dead: now therefore arise, go over this Jordan, thou, and all this people, unto the land which I do give to them, even to the children of Israel. (Joshua 1:1–2)

Joshua heard and obeyed the command of the Lord.

Enoch Walked with God

The father of Methuselah, a man that walked with God. And Enoch walked with God: and he was not; For God took him. (Genesis 5:24)

God did not allow Enoch to die. Enoch went to heaven (the presence of God) without dying.

Noah and the Flood

And it came to pass, when men began to multiply on the face of the earth, and daughters were born unto them. That the sons of God saw the daughters of men that they were fair; and they took them wives of all which they chose.

Somethings to Ponder

Who were these sons of God?
Were they ungodly kings?
Were they fallen angels?
Were they the descendants from the godly line of Adam from his son Seth?
Who were these daughters of men?
Were these women from the descendants of Adam as well?
Perhaps godless descendants of Cain?
What are your thoughts?

And the Lord said, My spirit shall not always strive with man, for that he also is flesh: Yet his days shall be an hundred and twenty years. There were giants in the earth in those days; and also after that, when the sons of God came unto the daughters of men, and they bare children to them, the same became mighty men which were old, men of renown.

Wickedness and Violence on Earth—The Judgment

And the Lord saw that the wickedness of man was great in the earth, and that every imagnation of the thought of his heart was only evil continually. And it repented the Lord that he had made man on the earth, and it grieved him at his heart. And the Lord said, I will destroy man whom I have created from the face of the earth; both man, and beast, and the creeping thing, and the fowls of the air, for it repenteth me that I have made them.

Then there is Noah, the grandson of Methuselah, a righteous man.

But Noah, found grace in the eyes of the Lord. These are the generations of Noah: Noah was a just man and perfect in his generations, and Noah walked with God. And Noah begat three sons, Shem, Ham, and Japheth. The earth also was corrupt before God, and the earth was filled with violence.

Noah—Also a Man of Faith and Obedience

And God said unto Noah, the end of all flesh is come before me, for the earth is filled with violence through them; and behold, I will destroy them with the earth. Make thee an ark of gopher wood; rooms shalt thou make in the ark, and shalt pitch it within and without pitch. And this is the fashion which thou shalt make it of: The length of the ark shall be three hundred cubits, the breadth of it fifty cubits, and the height of it thirty cubits.

It has been stated that the ark was the size of five football fields.

A window shalt thou make to the ark, and in a cubit shalt thou finish it above: and the door of the ark shalt thou set in the side thereof; with lower, second, and third stories shalt thou make it. And, behold, I, even I, do bring a flood of waters upon the earth, to destroy all flesh, wherein is the breath of life, from under heaven; and every thing that is in the earth shall die. But with thee will I establish my covenant; and thou shalt come into the ark, thou, and thy sons, and thy wife, and thy sons' wives with thee. And of every living thing of all flesh, two of every sort shalt thou bring into the ark, to keep them alive with thee; they shall be male and female. And take thou unto thee of all food that is eaten, and thou shalt gather it to thee; and it shall be for food for thee, and for them.

Noah Obeyed God

Thus did Noah; according to all that God commanded him, so did he. (Genesis 6:1–19, 21–22)

God Is Still in Control

And the Lord said unto Noah, come thou and all thy house into the ark; for thee have I seen righteous before me in this generation. (Genesis 7:1)

Are we living righteous lives before God today?

And they went in unto Noah into the ark, two and two of all flesh, wherein is the breath of life. And they that went in, went in male and female of all flesh, as God had commanded him, and the Lord shut him in. (Genesis 7:15–16)

The Lord Shut the Door

The people of Noah's day were eating, drinking, and marrying and giving in marriage until the day Noah entered into the ark (Matthew 24:38). The people in Noah's day laughed at Noah, they took Noah as a joke. On this Christian journey, have you ever been ridiculed? How many times?

It's Going to Rain!

The rain was upon the earth forty days and forty night. The entire human population was destroyed by water.

> All flesh died that moved upon the earth, both of fowl,
> and of cattle, and of beast, and of every creeping thing that
> creepeth upon the earth, and every man. (Genesis 7:21)

God was not happy having to curse the ground with water, and he said he would not destroy the earth again with water.

Only Noah and the seven others with him and the animals were saved.

Isaiah—Here Am I, Lord. Send Me!

> In the year King Uzziah died, I saw also the Lord sitting
> upon a throne, high and lifted up, and his train filled the
> temple. Above it stood the seraphims, each one has six
> wings; with twain he covered his face, and with twain he
> covered his feet, and with twain he did fly.

The Seraphims—Angelic Agents

> And one cried unto another, and said, Holy, holy, holy, is
> the Lord of hosts: the whole earth is full of his glory. And
> the posts of the door moved at the voice of him that cried,
> and the house was filled with smoke.

Isaiah examined himself, saw his predicament, and wanted to do something about it.

> Then said I, Woe is me! for I am undone; because I am a man of unclean lips, and I dwell in the midst of a people of unclean lips: for mines eyes have seen the King, the Lord of hosts. Then flew one of the seraphims unto me, having a live coal in his hand, which he had taken with the tongs from off the altar; And he laid it upon my mouth, and said, Lo, this hath touched thy lips, and thine iniquity is taken away, and thy sin purged.

Cleansed by God

> Also I heard the voice of the Lord, saying, Whom shall I send, and who will go for us? Then said I, Here am I, send me.

We can clearly see the Trinity at work here.

Isaiah's Commission

> And he said, Go, and tell this people, Hear ye indeed, but understand not; and see ye indeed, but perceive not. (Isaiah 6:1–9)

Go, Isaiah, and tell even though the people might not take heed.

Our Suffering Savior

Isaiah found himself in the presence of God and received revelations from God to write Isaiah 53, which describes the future suffering of our Lord and Savior Jesus Christ.

> He was despised and rejected of men; a man of sorrows, acquainted with grief; and we hid as it were our faces from him: he was despised, and we esteemed him not.

But he was wounded for our transgressions, he was bruised for our iniquities: the chastisement of our peace was upon him, and with his stripes we are healed.

And he made his grave with the wicked, and with the rich in his death; because he had done no violence, neither was any deceit in his mouth.

Yet, it pleased the Lord to bruise him; he hath put him to grief: when thou shalt make his soul an offering for sin, he shall see his seed, he shall prolong his days, and the pleasure of the lord shall proper in his hand. (Isaiah 53:3, 5, 9, 10)

It pleased God to bruise him for us. God gave his only begotten Son. But Christ's own people rejected their Messiah, the one they had been waiting anxiously for.

And they cried out all at once, saying, Away with this man, and release unto us Barabbas: (Who for a certain sedition made in the city, and for a murder, was cast into prison. Pilate therefore, willing to release Jesus, spake again to them. But they cried, saying, crucify him, crucify him. (Luke 23:18–21)

Jesus Christ, one who healed the sick, fed the hungry, and raised the dead found himself in the hands of sinful men. Christ still gave his life for us because he loved us and our fellowship and wanted us to be in his presence for eternity.

The description below can also reference what happened to Christ at the hands of his so-called friends.

Wounds

And one shall say unto him, what are these wounds in thine hands? Then he shall answer, Those with which I was wounded in the house of my friends. (Zechariah 13:6)

Thomas the Disciple and the Wounds of Christ

> The other disciples therefore said unto him, We have seen
> the Lord. But he said unto them, Except I shall see in his
> hands the print of the nails, and put my finger into the
> print of the nails, and thrust my hand into his side, I will
> not believe. And after eight days again his disciples were
> within, and Thomas with them: then came Jesus, the
> doors being shut, and stood in the midst, and said, Peace
> be unto you. Then saith he to Thomas, Reach hither
> thy finger, and behold my hands; and reach hither thy
> hand, and thrust it into my side, and be not faithless, but
> believing. And Thomas answered and said unto him, My
> Lord and my God. Jesus saith unto him, Thomas, because
> thou hast seen me, thou hast believed: blessed are they
> that have not seen, and yet have believed. (John 20:25–29)

The reference is to us, Christians, the body of Christ. When we see
Jesus, he will still bear the marks of the cross.

Can you relate to this?

> For God so loved the world, that he gave his only begotton
> Son, that whosoever believeth in him should not perish,
> but have everlasting life. (John 3:16)

Jonah

Jonah, a selfish and disobedient preacher, found himself in the midst
of a storm. Due to his lack of knowledge, he thought he could hide from
the presence of God.

The Lord had commanded Jonah to go and preach to the people of
Nineveh because of their wickedness, but Jonah hated those people and
did not want them to be saved.

Do we want all men to be saved and go to heaven? Our answer should
be yes.

But what about those who have injured and mocked us? Remember what God said about vengeance being his.

> But Jonah rose up to flee unto Tarshish from the Presence of the Lord, and went down to Joppa; and he found a ship going to Tarshish: so he paid the fare thereof, and went down into it, to go with them unto Tarshish from the Presence of the Lord. (Jonah 1:2–3)

The Lord Caused Jonah's Storm

God was still in control; obedience is better than sacrifice.

> But the Lord sent out a great wind into the sea, and there was a mighty tempest in the sea, so that the ship was like to be broken. Then the mariners were afraid, and cried every man unto his god, and cast forth the wares that were in the ship into the sea, to lighten it of them. But Jonah was gone down into the the sides of the ship; and he lay, and was fast asleep. So the shipmaster came to him, and said unto him, What meanest thou, O sleeper? arise, call upon thy God, if so be that God will think upon us, that we perish not.

Casting Lots

> And they said every one to his fellow, Come, and let us cast lots, that we may know for whose cause this evil is upon us. So they cast lots, and the lot fell upon Jonah.

Who Are You?

> Then said they unto him, Tell us, we pray thee, for whose cause this evil is upon us: What is thine occupation? and whence comest thou? What is thy country? And of what people art thou? And he said unto them, I am an Hebrew; and I fear the Lord, the God of heaven, which hath made

the sea and the dry land. Then were the men exceedingly afraid, and said unto him, Why hast thou done this? For the men knew that he fled from the Presence of the Lord, because he had told them. (Jonah 1:4–10)

Jonah Thrown Overboard

We all know the story how Jonah was thrown overboard by the sailors at his request because of the storm beating upon the boat. When Jonah was thrown overboard, the sea ceased from its raging (Jonah 1:12–17).

A Whale!

God had prepared a big fish to swallow Jonah.

For as Jonas was three days and three nights in the whale's belly; so shall the Son of man be three days and three nights in the heart of the earth. (Matthew 12:40)

Jonah was indeed in the belly of the whale three days and three nights according to scripture.

Jonah knew he was in trouble, a type of hell.

Then Jonah prayed unto the Lord his God out of the fish's belly, And said, I cried by reason of mine affliction unto the Lord, and he heard me; out of the belly of hell cried I, and thou heardest my voice. (Jonah 2:1–2)

I will look again toward thy holy temple, I will give God the Thanksgiving and the Praise, I will obey God as I have promised.

God is waiting and listening for our submission. He still answers prayers.

And the Lord spake unto the fish and it vomited out Jonah upon dry land. (Jonah 2:10)

Finally, Jonah said yes to the Lord and did what God had commanded him to do. Repentance was the consequence of Jonah's preaching.

> So, the people of Nineveh believed God, and proclaimed a fast, and put on sackcloth, from the greatest of them even to the least of them.

> And God saw their works, that they turned from their evil way; and God repented of the evil, that he had said he would do unto them, and did it not. (Jonah 3:5, 10)

God is still in charge, and he is still merciful.

Elijah Proclaimed—Choose This Day Whom You Will Serve

God sent Elijah the prophet to confront the apostasy of the children of Israel and Baal worship.

> And Elijah came unto all the people, and said, how long shalt ye between two opinion? if the Lord be God, follow him: but if Baal, then follow him. And the people answered him not a word. Then said Elijah unto the people, I, even I only, remain a prophet of the Lord; but Baal's prophets are four hundred and fifty men.

Elijah's Challenge

> Let them therefore give us two bullocks; and let them choose one bullock for themselves, and cut it in pieces, and lay it on wood, and put no fire under: and I will dress the other bullock, and lay it on wood, and put no fire under.

Call upon Your God

> And call ye on the name of your gods, and I will call on the name of the Lord: and the God that answereth by fire, let him be God. And all the people answered and said, It

is well spoken. And Elijah said unto the prophets of Baal, Choose you one bullock for yourselves, and dress it first; for ye are many; and call on the name of your gods, but put no fire under. And they took the bullock which was given them, and they dressed it, and called on the name of Baal from morning even until noon, saying, O Baal, hear us. But there was no voice, nor any that answered. And they leaped upon the altar which was made.

The Prophets of Baal Damaged the Altar in Their Anger

And it came to pass at noon, that Elijah mocked them, and said, Cry aloud: for he is a god; either he is talking, or he is pursuing, or he is in a journey, or peradventure he sleepeth, and must be awaked. And they cried aloud, and cut themselves after their manner with knives and lancets, till the blood gushed out upon them. And it came to pass, when midday was past, and they prophesied until the time of the offering of the evening sacrifice, that there was neither voice, nor any to answer, nor any that regarded.

The Prophets of Baal Put on Their Show from Noon until Three

And Elijah said unto all the people, Come near unto me. And all the people came near unto him. And he repaired the altar of the Lord that was broken down.

Jacob had twelve sons, and God named Jacob Israel.

And Elijah took twelve stones, according to the number of the tribes of the sons of Jacob, unto whom the word of the Lord came, saying, Israel shall be thy name: And with the stone he built an altar in the name of the Lord: and he made a trench about the altar, as great as would contain two measures of seed. An he put the wood in order, and cut he bullock in pieces, and laid him on the wood, and said, Fill your barrels with water, and pour it on the burnt sacrifice, and on the wood. And he said, Do it the second time, And they did it the second time. And he said, Do it the third time. And they did it the third time. And the water ran round about the altar; and he filled the trench also with water.

God Shows Up

And it came to past at the time of the offering of the evening sacrifice, that Elijah the prophet came near, and said, Lord God of Abraham, Isaac, and of Israel, let it be known this day that thou art God in Israel, and that I am thy servant, and that I have done all these things at thy word. Hear me, o Lord, hear me, that this people may know that thou art the Lord God, and that thou has turned their heart back again. Then, the fire of the Lord fell, and consumed the burnt sacrifice, and the wood, and the stones, and the dust, and licked up the water that was in the trench. And when all the people saw it, they fell on their faces: and they said, the Lord, he is the God: the Lord, he is the God.

False Prophets Will Not Escape the Judgment of God

And Elijah said unto them, Take the prophets of Baal; let not one of them escape. And they took them: and Elijah brought them down to the brook kishon, and slew them there. (1 Kings 18:21–40)

The list above contains just a few of the obedient servants of God who enjoyed his presence and said yes to God's call.

Are you one of them?

CHAPTER 5

༄

WOMEN OF GOD
MAKING A STAND

The Old Testament mentions prophetesses a number of times. A prophetess is a woman who exercised the prophetic gift in ancient Israel or in the early Christian church. There are at least four women I came across in the Old Testament who carried that mark. There are more, but these four grabbed my attention.

Miriam

Miriam was the elder sister of Aaron and Moses, a servant of God. She played a part in assisting Moses and Aaron with the Hebrews during their transition from slavery.

Musical Talent

A celebration of song and dance to the Lord was their answer for their deliverance from the hands of the Egyptians.

> And Miriam, the prophetess, the sister of Aaron, took a timbrel in her hand: and all the women went out after her with timbrels and with dances. And Miriam answered them, Sing ye to the Lord, for he hath triumphed

gloriously; the horse and his rider hath he thrown into the sea. (Exodus 15:20–21)

Miriam was referring to Pharaoh's army.

God's Command to Moses, Aaron, and Miriam

And the Lord spake suddenly unto Moses, and unto Aaron, and Miriam, Come out ye three unto the tabernacle of the congregation. And they three came out.

God in the Pillar of Cloud

And the Lord came down in the pillar of the cloud, and stood in the door of the tabernacle and called Aaron and Miriam: and they both came forth. And he said, Hear now my words: if there be a prophet among you, I the Lord will make myself known unto him in a vision, and will speak unto him in a dream. My servant Moses is not so, who is faithful in all mine house.

With him will I speak mouth to mouth, even apparently, and not in dark speeches; and the similitude of the Lord shall he behold: wherefore then were ye not afraid to speak against my servant Moses? (Numbers 12:4–8)

Be careful not to speak evil of God's servants!

And the cloud departed from off the tabernacle; and, behold, Miriam became leprous, white as snow: and Aaron looked upon Miriam, and, behold, she was leprous. (Numbers 12:10)

Miriam, Moses's sister, was struck with leprosy for speaking evil of him for marrying the Ethiopian woman. God was advising the siblings that he spoke to Moses openly and directly. But for prophets, visions and dreams were used as well.

Israel's Deliverance by Deborah and Barak

> Deborah, a prophetess, a military heroine, the wife of
> Lap'idoth, a judge of Israel. And she sent and called Barak
> the son of Abin'oam out of Kadesh-naph'tali, and said
> unto him, hath not the Lord God of Israel commanded,
> saying, Go and draw toward Mount Tabor, and take with
> thee ten thousand men of the children of Naph'tali and
> of the children of Zebu'lun. And I will draw unto thee to
> the river Kishon Sisera, the captain if Jabin's army, with
> his chariot and his multitude, and I will deliver him into
> thine hand. (Judges 4:4, 6–7)

God spoke through Deborah, a woman, informing her what to tell
Barak. Barak was to attack the Canaanites, and Deborah was to accompany
him. God helped Deborah and Barak defeat the Canaanites.

Hildah—Spokesperson for God

> So Hilki'ah the priest, and Ahi'kam, and Ach'bor, and
> Sha'phan, and Asahi'ah, dah, went unto Huldah the
> prophetess, the wife of Shallum the son of Tikyah, the
> of Har'has, keeper of the wardrobe; (now she dewell in
> Jerusalem in the college;) and they communed with her.
>
> And she said unto them, Thus said the Lord, the God of
> Israel, Tell the man that sent you to me, Thus said the
> Lord, behold, I will bring evil upon this place, and upon
> the inhabitants thereof, even all the words of the book
> which the King of Judah hath read. (2 Kings 22:14–17)

The people had forsaken God and had burned incense to other strange
gods.

The Unnamed Wife of Isaiah

> Moreover the Lord said unto me, Take thee a great roll, and write in it with a man's pen concerning Ma'her-shal'al-hash-baz. And I took unto me faithful witnesses to record, Uri'ah the priest, and Zechariah the son of Jeberechi'ah. And I went unto the prophetess; and she conceived, and bare a son. Then said the Lord to me, Call his name Ma'her-shal'al-hash'-baz. (Isaiah 8:1–3)

Ma'her-sha'al-hash'-baz, Isaiah's second son, has a name that means "quick pickings," "easy prey."

Thank God for these prophetesses!

Let's look at other God-fearing women of old.

Queen Esther

With the aid of her cousin, Mordeca'i, Queen Esther helped deliver her people, the Jews, in Persia and Media by boldly telling the king, her husband, about Haman's plot to kill the Jews.

> Also Vashti the queen made a feast for the women in the royal house which belonged to King Ahausue'rus.

> The king wanted to show off his wife's beauty.

> He ordered the seven chamberlains to bring Vashti the Queen before the King with the crown royal, to shew the people and the princes her beauty: for she was fair to look on.

> The queen refused, and the king was wroth. A decree was written.

> Queen Vashti would not come before the King again, her royal estate would be given to another that was better than she.

The decree was to be published throughout all his empire, for it was great. All wives shall give to their husbands honour, both great and small.

Fair young virgins were sought for the king.

So Esther was taken unto King Ahasue'rus into his house royal in the tenth month, which is the month Tebeth, in the seventh year of his reign.

And the King loved Esther above all the women, and she obtained grace and favour, in his sight more than all the virgins, so that he set the royal crown upon her head, and made her queen instead of Vashti. (Esther 1:9, 11–12, 16–17, 20, 2:2, 17)

All Things Work Together for the Good

God's name is not mentioned in the book of Esther, but we do know God was in control and still cared for his chosen people.

Behold, he that keepeth Israel shall neither slumber nor sleep. (Psalm 121:4)

Ruth

The author of the book of Ruth is unknown. A number of theologians have accredited the writing to Samuel.

In Ruth 1, we read of a woman named Ruth, a Gentile who was also a Moabite. Ruth loved her mother-in-law, Naomi, a righteous woman whose name meant "pleasant" or "my joy."

Naomi's lost her husband and two sons, Mahlon and Chilion. Ruth, after the death of her husband, chose to remain with Naomi even after being dismissed by Naomi to return to her mother's house.

And Ruth said, Entreat me not to leave thee, or to return from following after thee: for whither thou goest, I will

go; and where thou lodgest, I will lodge: thy people shall
be my people, and thy God my God. (Ruth 1:16)

That was a beautiful statement of commitment. Have you ever heard
these words expressed in wedding ceremonies? Ruth was leaving her beliefs
and way of life to follow the beliefs, vows, and customs of her mother-in-
law. Ruth really brought it home when she stated that Naomi's God would
be her God as well.

Naomi resented God for her troubles.

So they two went until they came to Bethlehem. And it
came to pass, when they were come to Bethlehem, that
all the city was moved about them, and they said, Is this
Naomi? And she said unto them, Call me not Naomi, call
me Mara: For the almighty hath dealt very bitterly with
me. I went out full, and the Lord hath brought me home
again empty: why then call ye me Naomi, seeing the Lord
hath testified against me, and the almighty hath afflicted
me? (Ruth 1:19–21)

In the book of Ruth, we find a partial lineage of King David and
Christ. We can clearly see Gentile blood in the lineage of Christ.

Boaz Meets Ruth

Boaz, a kinsman of Naomi's husband, was a mighty man of wealth of
the family of Elimelech (Ruth 2:1).

So Boaz took Ruth, and she was his wife: and when he
went in unto her, the Lord gave her conception, and she
bare a son. And Naomi took the child, and laid it in her
bosom, and became a nurse unto it.

And the women her neighbours gave it a name, saying,
There is a son born to Naomi: and they called his name
Obed: he is the father of Jesse, the father of David. (Ruth
4:13, 16–17)

NEW TESTAMENT WOMEN OF GOD (TO NAME A FEW)

Anna—A Prophetess

> And there was one Anna, a prophetess, the daughter of Phanuel of the tribe of Aser. She was of great age, and had lived with an husband seven years from her virginity. And she was a widow of about fourscore and four years, which departed not from the temple, but served God with fastings and prayers night and day. And she coming in that instance gave thanks likewise unto the Lord, and spake of him to all them that looked for redemption in Jerusalem. (Luke 2:36–38)

Lydia—A Missionary Woman

> And a certain woman named Lydia, a seller of purple, of the city of Thyatira, which worshipped God, heard us: that she attended unto the things which were spoken of Paul. And when she was baptized, and her household, she besought us, saying, If ye have judged me to be faithful to the Lord, come into my house, and ABIDE there. And she constrained us. (Acts 16:14–15)

Phoebe—A Deaconess

Phoebe was a deaconess in the church at Cenchreae according to Paul. She was a helper to many including Paul.

> I commend unto you Phebe our sister, which is a servant of the church which is at Cenchrea: That ye receive her in the Lord, as becometh saints, and that ye assist her in whatsoever business she hath need of you: for she hath been a succourer of many, and of myself also. (Romans 16:1–2)

Paul's Comments on the Wives of Deacons

> Even so must their wives be grave, not slanderers, sober,
> faithful, in all things. (1 Timothy 3:11)

Paul's helpers risked their lives for him.

> Greet Priscilla and Aquila my helpers in Christ Jesus.

Priscilla explained the gospel to Apollos more accurately. Apollos was a Jew who knew more about the baptism of John.

> Who have for my life laid down their own necks: unto
> whom not only I give thanks, but also all the churches of
> the Gentiles. (Romans 16:3–4)

Philip's Four Daughters

In the New Testament, Philip the evangelist was said to have four unmarried daughters who prophesied. During the awakening of the early church, a number of believers were given the gift of prophecy. The revelation was the direction for the church to go. The revelation was given with the aid of the Holy Spirit, the presence of God, before the New Testament was completed.

> And the next day we that were of Paul's company departed,
> and came unto caesare'a and we entered into the house of
> Philip the evangelist, which was one of the seven; and
> abode with him. And the same man had four daughters,
> virgins, which did prophesy. (Acts 21:8–9)

Prophesy again is the telling of divine inspiration. We can clearly see the variety of gifts exhibited by these women of faith and co-laborers in the early church.

Women play a major role in the spreading of the gospel and standing on the promises of God in this new era as well.

CHAPTER 6

WHO KNOWS THE WAYS OF A WOMAN?

Do you remember the capable wife? She was called a virtuous woman. Virtuous reference to showing strength, ability, wealth, and valor and being efficient. This woman was excellent in every way, and most important, she was God fearing. The virtuous woman found favor with God and was precious in his sight. The virtuous woman's husband safely trusted her. That is an attribute that is truly a blessing then and now. In any relationship, if there is no trust, there probably is not much of a relationship.

A number of us have accredited King Lemuel with the question "Who can find a virtuous woman? For her price is far above rubies" (Proverbs 31:10).

King Lemuel was a man taught by his mother; she did a wonderful job.

We do know rubies are precious. A virtuous woman has worth.

Let's look at the word *anointed.* We come across the meanings holy and appointed of God to serve. Therefore, the virtuous woman exhibits the fruits of being

1. a saved woman;
2. an obedient woman;
3. a loving woman;
4. a kind woman;
5. a woman who speaks no evil of others on purpose;

6. a woman who is not two-faced;
7. a woman who is not a backbiter;
8. a woman who can be trusted;
9. a woman who is no respecter of persons; she does not love some people but loves everyone and gives everyone a chance;
10. a woman who is long-suffering and patient;
11. a woman who is not jealous or afraid of other Christians women's gifts;
12. a woman of strength, faith, and firm beliefs;
13. a woman who knows when to speak and when to be quiet;
14. a woman who trains her children in the knowledge of God;
15. a woman who works hard at taking care of her husband's and children's needs and her home;
16. a woman who submits to her husband; and
17. a woman who sets the tune for her home.

An unhappy woman can make a home not so homey, and no one will be dancing to any tunes.

The key to the virtuous woman beauty lies in her spiritual life with God. We call that beauty the Holy Spirit that dwells in women of God that makes us precious in the sight of God.

Marriage

Ladies, is it necessary to have God's presence in our marriages? You better believe it! The presence of God in the virtuous woman's marriage makes it easy for her to submit.

Should we obey the scriptures or not?

> Wives, submit yourselves unto your own husbands as unto the Lord. For the husband is the head of the wife, even as Christ is the head of the church; and he is the savior of the body. Therefore, as the church is subject unto Christ, so let the wives be to their own husbands in every thing.

Most of us women can stand a little more work on submitting to our own husbands. Ladies, do you agree? Or are you passing the test with flying colors?

I recall a pastor stating one day that it was easy for a woman to submit to her husband. He said that all we women needed to do was obey God and submit. I thought, *That's easy for you to say. You're not a woman!*

> Husbands, love your wives, even as Christ also loved the church, and gave himself for it. (Ephesians 5:22–25)

Christ died for the church. now that's what you call love!

> Whoso findeth a wife findeth a good thing, and obtaineth favour of the Lord. (Proverbs 18:22)

Are women to go out looking for husbands? What are your thoughts? Husbands are to love their wives as they love their own bodies. Therefore, if a husband loves his wife, he loves himself.

Remember what Adam said about the woman in the garden.

> This is now bone of my bones, and flesh of my flesh: she shall be called woman, because she was taken out of man. (Genesis 2:23)

Husbands and wives belongs to each other. Marriage is a holy institution established by God. He considers marriage a sacred bond, and he expects us to honor that union with lasting commitment. Faithfulness should exist between husband and wife. God honors faithfulness and trust, but God hates unfaithfulness.

Submission

Once a wife finds out that she has her husband's heart, that can make it easier for her to submit to him. Am I right?

If the wife knows beyond a shadow of doubt that her husband loves her, has her best interests at heart, and is trustworthy, she can trust him to do what is best without sinning against God and her. That makes submission easier.

We wives are to submit to the leadership of our husbands in everything. If the wife knows that her husband will not hurt himself, she knows that he loves her as he loves himself, and she will not be hurt intentionally by her husband. Submission should fall right in line with God's word. Amen?

We remember how Eve was deceived by the serpent but Adam was not. Nonetheless, he went along with the program. I wonder why.

We Women

> Notwithstanding she shall be saved in childbearing, if they continue in faith and charity and holiness with sobriety. (1 Timothy 2:14–15)

> Unto the woman he said, I will greatly multiply thy sorrow and thy conception, in sorrow thy shall bring forth children, and thy desire shall be to thy husband, and he Shall rule over thee. (Genesis 3:16)

Heed that word *rule*! This is the Word of God. We are to respect our husbands, love them, and live with them until death do us part. In this modern society, we find this vow is not always the case. God never changes, but people do! Sometimes the husband changes, or sometimes the wife changes. If we love God, we must pray often for our marriages and do our best to obey God in everything. No, it will not always be easy.

> Therefore, shall a man leave his father and his mother and shall cleave unto his wife; and they shall be one flesh. (Genesis 2:24)

A man must do what? Cleave to his wife. Okay! The scripture did not say anything about a man cleaving to his father and mother, sister or brother, nieces, nephews, or another man, or a woman friend but to cleave to his wife.

Are you with me, ladies?

> What God has joined together, let not man put asunder.
> (Mark 10:6–9)

What God has joined together, be careful … Do not interfere with it!

Have you ever had so-called friends, coworkers, in-laws, or family members get involved in your marriage? Remember, there are consequences for getting involved in other people's marriages in terms of causing conflicts. We must work hard not to be troublemakers in others' marriages. One consequence is to answer to God for our part because God is ever so present. Remember, we reap what we sow.

Please do not forget Miriam, the sister of Moses and Aaron. Miriam had a problem with Moses's wife, but in the end, she paid a huge price for speaking evil of Moses's wife.

God hates divorce, right? Some folks have used their spouses' infidelity as grounds for divorce, and some Christians have been deserted by unbelieving spouses, and still others suffered physical or emotional abuse and divorced for that reason. Remember that marriage is so important that both partners should try all necessary, holy, lawful means to preserve it. If outside help is needed, please seek this help from professional doctors, Holy Spirit–filled members from church, who have the couple's best interest at heart.

Please do not be quick to share precious matters and details of your marriage with so-called friends or relatives who means you harm. Some people focus on a married couple's situation to drive a wedge between the husband and wife. There is never enough room in a marriage for a third person whether family or friend.

A man's best friend should be his wife. A woman's best friend should be her husband.

Every marriage, person, and situation is different! My problem may not be yours.

The most important person to seek help and guidance from in any marriage is God! Invite the presence of God in your marriage today if you have not already done so.! The Holy Spirit should always be a welcoming third presence in all marriages.

CHAPTER 7

❧

THE LAW

Most of us learned the Ten Commandments in Sunday school. As a Sunday school superintendent and Sunday school teacher, I made sure all my students learned and could recited the Ten Commandments. God gave them to Moses to reveal to the children of Israel, God's chosen people; they were his expectations of them. The children of Israel had been delivered by the mighty hand of God using his servant Moses and Aaron, Moses's brother, remember?

The Children of Israel

> The Lord spake on this wise, That his seed should so-journ
> in a strange land; and that they should bring them into
> bondage, and entreat them evil for 400 year. (Acts 7:6)

The chosen people needed to know that God was righteous and holy and that as his chosen people, they too were to live holy lives. God was their God; they should not worship or serve any other god. They were to write these laws upon their hearts and teach them to their children.

They were no longer the slaves of Pharaoh, but they still had responsibilities to God. He wanted the children of Israel to know that he was the one who had brought them out of the land of Egypt, that he was their God, and that they were his people.

They were to be a kingdom of priests and a holy nation. But before God made his appearance to the people, they had to clean their bodies and clothes and be confined to camp at the nether part of Mount Sinai. Therefore, barriers were placed around the mountain.

The Lord came down upon Mount Sinai on the top of the mountain and spoke to Moses (Exodus 19:6, 10, 17, 20). Therefore, the children of Israel were to follow the Ten Commandments (Exodus 20:3–17).

Thou shall have no other gods before me.
Thou shall not worship any graven image.
Thou shall not take God's name in vain.
Remember the sabbath to keep it holy
Honor your father and mother.
Thou shall not kill.
Thou shall not commit adultery
Thou shall not steal
Thou shall not bear false witness against thy neighbor.
Thou shall not covet.

Can you see the handiwork of God? God was ever so present in the giving of the law. As hard as they tried, the children of Israel, God's chosen people, could not keep the law. The catch is that if you break one of them, you are already in trouble with the others; sin is sin.

> For whosoever shall keep the whole Law, and yet offend
> in one point, he is guilty of all. (James 2:10)

A fellow Christian once told me, "I do not commit adultery." My response was, "That's really good, but when was the last time you lied?"

> For all have sinned and come short of the glory of God.
> (Romans 3:23)

The apostle Paul stated it best when he wrote, "For that which I do I allow not: for what I would, that do I not; but what I hate, that do I. If then I do that which I would not, I consent unto the law that it is good."

The Old Nature vs. the New Nature

> Now then it is no more I that do it, but sin that dwelleth in me. For I know that in me (that is, in my flesh,) dwelleth no good thing: for to will is present with me; but how to perform that which is good I find not. For the good that I would I do not: but the evil which I would not, that I do. Now if I do that I would not, it is no more I that do it, but sin that dwelleth in me.

Am I speaking to someone today? Yes, and that includes me.

> I find than a law, that, when I would do good, evil is present with me. For I delight in the law of God after the inward man. But I see another law in my members, warring against the law of my mind, and bringing me into captivity to the law of sin which is in my members.

Jesus Paid the Price

> O wretched man that I am! Who shall deliver me from the body of this death?

Jesus Christ.

> I thank God through Jesus Christ our Lord. So then with the mind I myself serve the law of God; but with the flesh the law of sin. (Romans 7:15–25)

My sin may not be your sin, but I have done something wrong even if it was just sitting at the dinner table overeating. We all have skeletons in our closets.

> What then? shall we sin, because we are not under the law, but under grace? God forbid. (Romans 6:15)

The commandments came from God, who forbids us to go around sinning. God still must be first in our lives. He still requires us to love our neighbors. We still should not lie, steal, kill, covet, and so on. Because we could not keep the law, God provided a more excellent way for us, and that is Jesus!

Remember, the Ten Commandments are God's Word, which does not change.

The children of Israel needed an animal sacrifice often, but Jesus was the perfect sacrifice once and for all.

Master

Just one master should exist in our lives, and that master should be Jesus.

> Know you not, that to whom ye yield yourselves servants to obey, his servants ye are to whom ye obey, whether of sin unto death, or of obedience unto righteousness. (Romans 6:16)

Jesus Set Us Free from the Law

The law was perfect, but the flesh was weak. The law pointed toward Christ. According to Paul, the law was the great teacher.

> Wherefore the law was our schoolmaster to bring us into Christ, that we might be justified by faith. But after faith is come, we are no longer under a schoolmaster. For ye are all the children of God by faith in Christ Jesus. For as many of you as have been baptized into Christ have put on Christ. There is neither Jew nor Greek, there is neither bond nor free, there is neither male nor female: for ye are all one in Christ Jesus. And if ye be Christ's then are ye Abraham's seed, and heirs according to the promise. (Galatians 3:24–29)

The Presence of God

We are all children of God by his grace and our faith and belief in the finished work of Jesus Christ.

> Therefore we conclude that a man is justified by Faith without the deeds of the Law. (Romans 3:28)

The Law and a Curse

> Christ hath redeemed us from the curse of the law, being made a curse for us: For it is written, Cursed is every one that hangeth on a tree. (Galatians 3:13)

Did not our Lord hang on a tree? Again, Jesus paid the price. Well, what about Malachi 3:8–9? I'm glad you asked.

> Will a man rob God? Yet ye have robbed me. but ye say, Wherein have we robbed thee? In tithes and offerings. Ye are cursed with a curse: for ye have robbed me, even this whole nation.

The Jews and the priests had backslidden; they had forsaken their attempt to keep the law. They were lax in worship and tithing. This royal priesthood was in default.

One tithe was for the Levite priesthood, and a second tithe that was kept at home was taken for the poor and widowers. This second tithe was also used for the Lord's feast (Deuteronomy 14:22, 28–29).

Are we in default today? Remember, we all fall short one way or another. We are all guilty of robbing God of something. Sometimes, it can be something as simple as our spending time with God (fellowshipping, praying, and studying of the Word).

Almsgiving Not to Be Seen by Man

> Take heed that ye do not your alms before man, to be seen of them: otherwise ye have no reward of your Father which is in heaven. (Matthew 6:1)

Paul's Stand on Giving

> Every man according as he purposeth in his heart, so let
> him give; not grudgingly, or of necessity: for God loveth
> a cheerful giver. (2 Corinthians 9:7)

God loves a what? A cheerful giver.

Now look. If you do not feel comfortable giving your money, keep it.
Do not allow anyone to put you on the spot or pressure you into giving.
If your heart is not in giving the money, keep it; God does not want it.
Most people come to church prepared to give. Common sense tells us that
we are to help with church finances. Let the Holy Spirit be your guide in
giving, and remember, we are not cursed anymore; the debt has been paid.

> For Christ is the end of the Law for righteousness to
> everyone that believeth. (Romans 10:4)

Christ provided grace and mercy. The church age is now in the
dispensation of grace.

What is grace?

I'm glad you asked.

Grace is God's unmerited favor; we do not deserve it, but he loves us
so much that he provided it anyway.

> For by Grace are ye saved through Faith, and that not of
> yourselves. It is the gift of God. Not of works, lest any
> man should boast. (Ephesians 2:8–9)

No matter how hard or how much you work, it still will not be enough
to save you. James clearly told us that we work because we are saved, not
to be saved.

Again, this great gift of salvation comes about at the time when one
does what?

> In whom ye also trusted, after that ye heard the word
> of truth, the gospel of yor salvation: In whom also after

that ye believed, ye were sealed with that Holy Spirit of promise. (Ephesians 1:13)

We are sealed until the day of redemption. Our salvation is secured. No one, not even ourselves, can take away our salvation. God saved us, not man! Some men will condemn you if they can.

Jesus said, "I came not to destroy the law, but to fulfill it."

Let no man therefore judge you in meat, or in drink, or in respect of a holyday, or of the new moon, or of the sabbath days. (Colossians 2:16)

Have you ever been judged for eating pork or been told you were assembling on the wrong day? Have you ever been led to believe that because you were not in church on certain days, especially during the coronavirus, that you were not a true child of God and that you lacked faith?

Be quick to refresh yourself on the above scripture!

No Condemnation

There is therefore now no condemnation to them which are in Christ Jesus, who walk not after the flesh, but after the Spirit. (Romans 8:1)

Now do we get it? Is this hard to understand? If it still is, ask a reliable person, someone you trust, to help your understanding after you pray to God for directions, wisdom, and understanding.

Is it possible for me to point my finger at anyone without several fingers bending back and pointing at me? For the law of the Spirit of life in Christ Jesus hath made me free from the law of sin and death.

Christ condemned sin in the flesh. (Romans 8:1–3)

Well, what about the Law of the land? Christians are to be law-abiding citizens just like everyone else, right?

In situations where the law violates God's law, we are to obey God rather than man. Be prepared to suffer the consequences or penalties for violations of the law of the land.

Jesus said to give Caesar the things that were his and to God the things that were God's (Matthew 22:21). If the law calls for paying taxes, driving the speed limit, etc., God wants us to be in compliance with the law of the land.

Remember, God is a just God. When he judges, he judges righteousness. He requires us to worship and praise him. He requires us to obey him and be his servants. We are to worship and praise God, no one else. We are obedient to God because we love him.

We serve our fellow man by helping him if we can and loving him. If our fellow man is in sin, hate the sin, do not partake in the sin, but love the person and attempt to lead him to Christ.

We should seek the presence of God in all we do, amen.

CHAPTER 8

⸙

GOD SENT HIS SON

Jesus—Our Lord and Savior

For God so loved the world that he gave his only begotten Son, that whosoever believeth in him should not perish, but have everlasting life. (John 3:16)

Mary—The Mother of Jesus

Mary was also known as Miryam of Nazareth, a virgin.

And in the sixth month the angel Gabriel was sent from God unto a city of Galilee, named Nazareth, To a virgin espoused to a man whose name was Joseph, of the house of David; and the virgin's name was Mary. And the angel came in unto her, and said, hail, thou that art highly favoured, the Lord is with thee; blessed are thou among women.

Ask yourself, *Am I in God's favor?*

And when she saw him, she was troubled at his saying, and cast in her mind what manner of salutation this should be. And the angel said unto her, Fear not, Mary: for thou has found favour with God. And, behold, thou shall conceive in thy womb, and bring forth a son, and shall call his name JESUS. He shall be great, and shall be called the son of the highest; and the Lord God shall give unto him the throne of his father David. And he shall reign over the house of Jacob for ever; and of his kingdom there shall be no end. Then, said Mary unto the angel, How shall this be, seeing I know not a man.

In other words, Mary was saying she was a virgin.

The Power of God's Presence

And the angel answered and said unto her, The Holy Ghost shall come upon thee, and the power of the Highest shall overshadow thee: therefore also that holy thing which shall be born of thee shall be called the Son of God. (Luke 1:26–35)

Elisabeth—The Mother of John the Baptist

Elisabeth was from Judea; she was a relative of Mary and the wife of Zacharias, a priest and the father of John the Baptist.

Sometimes, we need a family member, friend, or God-sent person to just sit, listen, and to hear our cries.

At this particular time in Mary's life, Elisabeth was a person that could relate to the miracle she would announce.

The Angel

And, behold, thy cousin Elisabeth, she hath also conceived a son in her old age: and this is the sixth month with her, who was called barren.

The blessing of God was upon these women. With God, nothing is impossible.

And Mary arose in those days, and went into the hill country with haste, into a city of Judah; And entered into the house of Zacharias, and saluted Elisabeth. And it came to pass, that when Elizabeth heard the salutation of Mary, the babe leaped in her womb: and Elisabeth was filled with the Holy Ghost. (Luke 1:36–37, 39–41, 44)

The babe in Elizabeth's womb, John the Baptist, leaped for joy. Praise God on high!

Now the birth of Jesus Christ was on the wise: When as his mother Mary was espoused to Joseph, before they came together, she was found with child of the Holy Ghost. Then Joseph her husband, being a just man, and not willing to make her a public example, was minded to put her away privily.

Betrothed

Mary was betrothed to Joseph, a man of the house of David. Betrothal was a mutual promise or a contract for a future marriage. Individuals representing the groom and bride were included in the negotiations of the contract.

The groom often placed a ring on the future bride's finger.

A change in plans by one of the partners was taken seriously, and a fine could have been instituted.

Joseph was willing to give Mary a bill of divorcement believing Mary had been unfaithful to him. How nice of Joseph not to run out and attempt to disgrace Mary's name. Mary's name would be on the lips of many gossipers then and now. Joseph could have had a public and humiliating divorce ending their betrothal. If Joseph had chosen to put Mary away secretly, Mary still would have had to return home in shame.

The Lord Took Care of Joseph

But while he thought on these things, behold, the angel of the Lord appeared unto him in a dream, saying, Joseph, thou son of David, fear not to take unto thee, Mary thy wife: for that which is conceived in her is of the Holy Ghost. And she shall bring forth a son, and thou shalt call his name JESUS, for he shall save his people from their sins. Now all of this was done, that it might be fulfilled which was spoken of the Lord by the Prophet, saying, Behold, a virgin shall be with child, and shall bring forth a son, and they shall call his name Emmanuel, which being interpreted is, God with us.

Joseph Obeyed the Lord

Then Joseph being raised from sleep did as the angel of the Lord had bidden him, and took unto him his wife.

Joseph did not exercise an intimate relationship with Mary until sometime after the birth of Jesus.

And knew her not till she had brought forth her firstborn son: and he called his name Jesus. (Matthew 1:18–25)

Pay Your Taxes

Joseph and Mary headed to Judaea, the city of David, which is called Bethlehem, because he was of the house and lineage of David, to pay taxes. Mary was great with child.

The Birth of Our Savior

And so it was, that, while they were there, the days were accomplished that should be delivered. And she brought forth her firstborn son, and wrapped him in swaddling clothes, and laid him in a manger; because there was no room for them in the inn. (Luke 2:6–7)

What a Glorious Celebration!

And there were in the same country shepherds abiding in the field, keeping watch over their flock by night. And, lo, the angel of the Lord came upon them, and the glory of the Lord shone round about them: and they were sore afraid. The angel said unto them, Fear not: for behold, I bring you good tidings of great joy, which shall be to all people. For unto you is born this day in the city of David a saviour, which is Christ the Lord. And this shall be a sign unto you; Ye shall find the babe wrapped in swaddling clothes lying in a manger. And suddenly there was with the angels a multitude of heavenly host praising God, and saying, "Glory to God in the highest, and on earth peace, good will toward men."

Looking for Baby Jesus

And it came to pass, as the angels were gone away from them into heaven, the shepherds said one to another, Let us now go even unto Bethlehem, and see this thing which is come to pass, which the Lord hath made know unto us. And they came with haste, and found Mary, and Joseph, and the babe lying in a manger. And when they had seen it, they made known abroad the saying which was told them concerning this child. (Luke 2:1–17)

Wise Men, Follow That Star

When Jesus was born in Bethlehem of Judaea in the days of Herod the King, behold there came wise men from the east to Jerusalem. Saying, "Where is he that is born King of the Jews? for we have seen his star in the east, and are come to worship him." A star in the East, went before the Wise Men, till it came and stood over where the young child was. The Wise Men rejoiced with exceeding great joy, a celebration of praise. And when they were come into the house, they saw the young child with Mary his mother, and fell down, and worshipped him: and when they had opened their treasures, they presented unto him gifts; gold, and frankincense, and myrrh.

Gifts Worthy of a King

The early church looked at gold as symbolic of Christ's deity (God and man), the frankincense of Christ's purity, and the myrrh of Christ's death. One of the uses of myrrh in those days was for embalming.

And being warned of God in a dream that they should not return to Herod, they departed into their own country another way. (Matthew 2:1–2, 9, 10–12)

Do you see the picture here? We know that King Herod did not wish to worship the child but to harm him.

Jesus is God's gift to you. Are you willing to accept God's gift of salvation today if you have not already done so?

Christ's Ministry

Christ's ministry was to restore Israel to God and to bring light and salvation to us Gentiles.

CHAPTER 9

℘

THE OLD RUGGED CROSS

"I will cling to the old rugged cross, and exchange it some day for a crown." We praise God for the words in this beautiful song by George Bennard. Throughout our Christian journey, many of us have been enlightened and encouraged by the words of this song and its heartfelt lyrics.

The Romans nailed criminals to a cross causing their death. What a terrible way to die! The Romans did not discriminate; they nailed our Savior, Jesus Christ, to a cross even though he had committed no crime.

Jesus Christ, our Lord and Savior, the son of God, went about doing good. Let's walk the dusty roads of Jerusalem with our Lord Jesus.

At a Feast in Jerusalem, Jesus Healed the Sick

> And certain man was there, which had an infirmity thirty and eight years. When Jesus saw him lie, and knew that he had been now a long time in that case, he saith unto him, Wilt thou be made whole? The impotent man answered him, Sir, I have no man, when the water is troubled, to put me into the pool: but while I am coming, another steppeth down before me. Jesus saith unto him, Rise, take up thy bed, and walk. And immediately the man was made whole, and took up his bed, and walked: and on the same day was the sabbath. (John 5:5–9)

Jesus Raised the Dead

And when he thus had spoken, he cried with a loud voice, Lazarus, come forth. And he that was dead came forth, bound hand and foot with graveclothes: and his face was bound about with a napkin. Jesus saith unto them, Loose him, and let him go. (John 11:43–44)

Jesus Fed the Hungry

And he commanded the multitude to sit down on the grass, and took the five loaves, and the two fishes, and looking up to heaven, he blessed, and brake, and gave the loaves to his disciples, and the disciples to the multitude. And they did all eat, and were filled: and they took up of the fragments that remained twelve baskets full. And they that had eaten were about five thousand men, beside women and children. (Matthew 14:19–21)

Jesus—A Comforter

And I will pray the Father, and he shall give you another Comforter, that he may abide with you for ever. Even the Spirit of truth; whom the world cannot receive, because it seeth him not, neither knoweth him: but ye know him; for he dwelleth with you, and shall be in you. I will not leave you comfortless, I will come to you. But the Comforter, which is the Holy Ghost, whom the Father will send in my name, he shall teach you all things, and bring all things to your remembrance, whatsoever I have said unto you. (John 14:16–18, 26)

Jesus Kept His Word

Greater love hath no man than this, that a man lay down his life for his friends. Friends of Jesus included; Lazarus,

Martha, and Mary. Ye are my friends, if ye do whatsoever I command you. (John 15:13–14)

Jesus on the Law

Think not that I am come to destroy the law, or the prophets: I am not come to destroy, but to fulfil. (Matthew 5:17)

Jesus on Love

When asked what was the great commandment in the law by a Pharisee, who also happened to be a lawyer, Jesus said,

Thou shalt love the Lord thy God with all thy heart, and with all thy soul, and with all thy mind. This is the first and great commandment. And the second is like unto it, Thou shalt love thy neighbour as thyself. On these two commandments hang all the law and the prophets. (Matthew 22:35–40)

Jesus on Prayer

And it came to pass, that, as he was praying in a certain place, when he ceased, one of his disciples said unto him, Lord, teach us to pray, as John also taught his disciples.

That John was John the Baptist.

The Model Prayer

And he said unto them, When ye pray, say, Our Father which art in heaven, Hallowed be thy name. Thy kingdom come. Thy will be done, as in heaven, so in earth. Give us day by day our daily bread. And forgive us our sins for we also forgive every one that is indebted to us. And lead us not into temptation; but deliver us from evil. (Luke 11:1–4)

It was the custom of that time for rabbis to compose special prayers. Jesus was a prime example.

The Lord's Prayer

Jesus prayed in John 17. This prayer has been called the high-priestly prayer. Jesus prayed for his own glorification, believers, unity of believers especially in the formation of the church, and more.

Jesus over Demons

A man in the country of the Gadarenes, came from among the tombs, met Jesus. This man had an unclean spirit. No man could contain this man, not even with chains. And always, night and day, he was in the mountains, and in the tombs, crying, and cutting himself with stones. But when he saw Jesus afar off, he ran and worshipped him, And cried with a loud voice, and said, What have I to do with thee, Jesus, thou son of the most high God? I adjure thee by God, that thou torment me not. For he said unto him, Come out of the man, thou unclean spirit! And he asked him, What is thy name? And he answered, saying, My name is Legion: for we are many. Now there was there nigh unto the mountains a great herd of swine feeding. And all the devils besought him, saying, Send us into the swine, that we may enter into them. And forthwith Jesus gave them leave. And the unclean spirits went out, and entered into the swine: and the herd ran violently down a steep place into the sea, (they were about two thousand;) and were choked in the sea. (Mark 5:1–9, 11–13)

Even pigs did not wish to be possessed by demons.

Jesus on Money

> Lay not up for yourselves treasures upon earth, where moth and rust doth corrupt, and where thieves break through and steal: But lay up for yourselves treasures in heaven, where neither moth nor rust doth corrupt, and where thieves do not break through nor steal: For where your treasure is, there will your heart be also. No man can serve two masters: for either he will hate the one, and love the other; or else he will hold to the one, and despise the other, Ye cannot serve God and mammon. (Matthew 6:19–21, 24)

Jesus Calmed the Storm

> And there arose a great storm of wind, and the waves beat into the ship, so that it was now full. And he was in the hinder part of the ship, asleep on a pillow: and they awake him, and say unto him, Master, carest thou not that we perish? And he arose, and rebuked the wind, and said unto the sea, Peace, be still. And the wind ceased, and there was a great calm. And he said unto them, Why are ye so fearful? How is it that ye have no faith? And they feared exceedingly, and said one to another, What manner of man is this, that even the wind and the sea obey him? (Mark 4:37–41)

"This too shall pass" is what the Holy Spirit whispered to me one day during the storm of the coronavirus pandemic, an unfamiliar storm to us. We have lost many; at the present time, we are working hard at staying isolated and keeping the quarantined at a distance. Our doctors and scientists are hard at work for a vaccine. Doctors predict that a vaccine will not be available for all infected persons until early 2021. In the meantime, we are still holding on to God's unchanging hand, the only person who holds and knows the future.

The storm Peter and the disciples were in was not designed to help Mother Nature. That storm was violent and angry. I think it was that Jesus, the Son of God, was aboard that ship. The wind was angry, the waves were angry, but they were not satisfied. Is not this storm, the coronavirus, causing fear and anger in our lives as well?

The church is still here! Therefore, according to scriptures, we are not in the tribulation period.

What have we done or not done to cause surfacing of this storm in our society? Only God knows the reason for this storm. Remember Job and his troubles?

Saints in the early church were scattered because of the fear of being persecuted by Saul. Several saints today are scattered because of the fear of contracting the virus, and I am no exception.

This enemy does not discriminate; it has no respect for people. Most of us believers in the household of faith are praying, "Help us, Lord!" lest we perish in the face of this unnatural storm.

Believers, keep Jesus on board in your life just like the disciples called on Jesus in their time of trouble in the midst of their storm. We know and trust that Jesus will never leave us in the midst of a storm. He has been faithful too many times in the past when we could not help or carry ourselves.

Can you count the times the Lord has commanded the wind to cease, and peace to be still in your life?

God said,

> Fear thou not; for I am with thee: be not dismayed;
> For I am thy God: I will strengthen thee; yea, I will
> help thee; Yea, I will uphold thee with the right hand of
> righteousness. (Isaiah 41:10)

God Never Changes

> For I am the Lord, I change not; therefore ye sons of Jacob
> are not consumed. (Malachi 3:6)

Are you a descendant of Abraham, Isaac, and Jacob? Don't fool me now!

Jesus the Messiah

> The woman saith unto him, I know that the Messiah cometh, which is called Christ: when he is come, he will tell us all things. Jesus saith unto her, I that speak unto thee am he. (John 4:25–26)

Jesus the Savior

> For God so loved the world that he gave his only begotten son, that whosoever believeth in him shall not perish, but have everlasting life. (John 3:16)

This same Jesus, our Lord, found himself in the company of evil men. Have you ever been in the presence of evil men or in the company of your enemies? It's not a good feeling, right?

David Wrote a Song of Trust

David wrote in Psalm 23:5, "Thou preparest a table before me in the presence of mine enemies: thou anointest my head with oil; my cup runneth over." He knew that the Lord was his shepherd who would be with him and provide his needs.

The Jews, God's chosen people, Jesus's own people, rejected their Messiah and cried, "Crucify him!" Picture yourself being rejected by your own people, your own church members turning on you.

Pilate, after finding no fault in Jesus, said, "But you have a custom, that I should release unto you one at the passover: will ye therefore that I release unto you the King of the Jews?"

Ain't nothing like a group of your own so-called people against you!

> Then cried they all again, saying not this man, but Barab'bas. Now barab'bas was a robber. (John 18:39–40)

> Then Pilate therefore took Jesus, and scourged him. (John 19:1)

Why?
Think about the word *prophecy.*
Think about the word *fear.*
Think about Satan and his lies.
Think about unbelief.
Think about being a King, the Son of God.
Think about being a friend to the world.
Think about position or status.

And the soldiers platted a crown of thorns, and put it on
his head, and they put on him a purple robe.

The word *platted* means woven. In those days, the color purple
symbolized royalty. Thorns as a crown ... Words cannot express how
painful this was for our Lord.

And said, hail, King of the Jews? and they smote him with
their hands.

Those evil men then mocked Jesus by asking him to identify the
person who had hit him.

When the chief priests therefore and officers saw him,
they cried out, saying, Crucify him, crucify him. Pilate
saith unto them, Take ye him, and crucify him: for I find
no fault in him. The Jews answered him, We have a law,
and by our law he ought to die, because he made himself
the Son of God. When Pilate therefore heard that saying,
he was the more afraid. And went again into the judgment
hall, and saith unto Jesus, Whence art thou? But Jesus
gave him no answer. Then saith pilate unto him, Speakest
thou not unto me? Knowest thou not that I have power
to crucify thee, and have power to release thee? Jesus
answered, Thou couldest have no power at all against me,
except it were given thee from above: therefore he that
delivered me unto thee hath the greater sin.

Jesus Was Rejected

> And from thenceforth Pilate sought to release him: but
> the Jews cried out, saying, If thou let this man go, thou
> art not Caesar's friend: whosoever maketh himself a king
> speaketh against Caesar. (John 19:1–3, 6–12)

So they crucified our Lord.

> And he bearing his cross went unto a place called the place
> of a skull, which is called in the Hebrew Gol'gotha: Where
> they crucified him, and two others with him, on either
> side one, and Jesus in the midst. (John 19:17–18)

Jesus was nailed to a rugged cross and was speared in his side. Jesus had
informed his enemies that if they tore the temple down, he would raise it
up again in three days. Jesus had also stated that no man takes his life; he
freely gives it, and if he lays it down, he can pick it back up.

Father, Forgive Them

> Then said Jesus, Father forgive them; for they know not
> what they do. And they parted his raiment and cast lots.
> (Luke 23:34)

A Criminal Speaks

> And one of the malefactors which were hanged railed on
> him, saying, If thou be Christ, save thyself and us. But the
> other answering rebuked him, saying, Dost not thou fear
> God, seeing thou art in the same condemnation? And we
> indeed justly; for we receive the due reward of our deeds:
> but this man hath done nothing amiss.

A Sinner Saved by Jesus on the Cross

> And he said unto Jesus, Lord, remember me when thou comest into thy kingdom. And Jesus said unto him, Verily I say unto thee, To day shalt thou be with me in paradise. And it was about the sixth hour (noon), and there was a darkness over all the earth until the ninth hour. And the sun was darkened, and the vail of the temple was rent in the midst.

The veil was the curtain in the temple that separated the holy of holies from other parts of the temple. God tore it. It meant that the new and living way was now open to the presence of God for all. Jesus had already said, "I am the way."

> And when Jesus had cried with a loud voice, he said, Father, into thy hands I commend my spirit, and having said, he gave up the ghost. (Luke 23:34, 39–46)

> Oh my Lord and my God!
> Remember, God was and still is in control!

Water Baptism

Notice that the malefactor was not baptized with water. He had no time to tarry for the Holy Spirit, and the scriptures mention nothing of him speaking in tongues. But Jesus promised him that he would be with him that day.

The Resurrection

But Jesus did not stay dead!

Women of Faith

We see faithful women on the scene.

> Now upon the first day of the week, very early in the
> morning, they came into the sepulchre, bringing the
> spices which they had prepared, and certain other with
> them. (Luke 24:1)

It was early Sunday morning, the first day of the week, not the Sabbath
Day. Mark said that these women were Mary Magdalene, Mary, the
mother of James, and Salo'me.

Remember, there was concern about the removal of the stone to gain
entrance to Jesus's tomb. But to their surprise, when they arrived, the stone
has already been rolled away. God can do anything!

Mary Magdalene

According to John, Mary Magdalene left with the message that the
Savior was missing from the sepulchre.

> Peter therefore went forth, and that other disciple, and
> came to the sepulchre. The disciples went away again,
> unto their own homes after seeing the napkins and linen
> clothes but not Jesus.

> But Mary stood without at the sepulchre weeping: and
> as she wept, she stooped down, and looked into the
> sepulchre. And seeing two angels in white sitting, the
> one at the head, and the other at the feet, where the body
> of Jesus had lain. And they say unto her, Woman, why
> weepest thou? She said unto them, Because they have
> taken away my Lord, and I know not where they have laid
> him. And when she had thus said, she turned herself back,
> and saw Jesus standing, and knew not that it was Jesus.

> Jesus saith unto her, Woman, why weepest thou? whom
> seekest thou? she, supposing him to be the gardener, saith
> unto him, Sir, if thou have borne him hence, tell me where
> thou hast laid him, and I will take him away.

Jesus saith unto her, Mary. She turned herself, and saith unto him, Rabbo'ni; which is to say, Master. Jesus saith unto her, Touch me not; for I am not yet ascended to my Father: but go to my brethren, and say unto them, I ascend unto my Father, and your Father; and to my God, and your God.

"Go and tell"—What a Mission!

Mary Magdalene came and told the disciples that she has seen the Lord, and that he has spoken these things unto her. (John 20:1–18)

A woman shared the good news of the resurrection of the son of God, and that mission for us Christians today has not changed.

How Is Your Walk with Christ?

Pray with me and assure me that you too are still walking with him. God, we praise you!

CHAPTER 10

❧

THE LOCAL CHURCH

Do you belong to one? Is the Comforter in operation there, or has the Holy Spirit been fired? The Holy Spirit dwells in saved believers, not in buildings made by hands, right?

School teachers regularly take attendance; students are either absent or present. When their names are called, some students say, "Present," some say, "Here," and others just raise their hands.

Most people are eager to join a church. They may at first feel a sense of belonging. Out of obedience, believers want to be present with the saints, and they are eager to continue rightly dividing the word of truth.

The physical church is a place filled with peaceful, kind, loving, Holy Spirit–filled, encouraging, and understanding people. Are you with me?

The New Testament church is an organized body of baptized believers. All members should have equal rights, privileges, and duties.

Christ Is the Head of the Church

It should be easy for believers to distinguish between a church established under the direction of the Holy Spirit and a church established by man.

The Lord's church is to deliver the gospel of Christ to all nations. Remember the Great Commission? The Lord's church is to be a place where we are to find fellowship, support, encouragement, and much love as we learn what God's expectations of us are just like the children of Israel when they received the Ten Commandments. This makes sense, right?

The church belongs God. Do you agree?

Let's see what Luke has to say about that.

> Take heed therefore unto yourselves, and to all the flock, over the which the Holy Ghost hath made you overseers, to feed the church of God, which he hath purchased with his own blood. (Acts 20:28)

The Holy Spirit has made us overseers, not owners, of the church. Jesus is the head of the church. He informed his disciples of his church during his ministry.

> And I say unto thee, That thou art Peter, and upon this rock I will build my church; and the gates of hell shall not prevail against it. (Matthew 16:18)

So God left man in charge to be faithful servants and stewards over his church. Are we still on the same page? The Holy Spirit should be our guide.

A number of churches have covenants, voluntary agreements in which members agree to conduct themselves in ways pleasing to God, to help with the upkeep and finances of the church, to assemble its members, to administer communion, see to the religious education of the children … The list goes on.

The denomination of a church is usually recognized by its doctrines—its beliefs and principles.

Who Do Men Say Jesus Was?

> When Jesus came into the coase of Caesare'a Philip'p, he asked his disciples, saying whom do men say that I the son of man am? And they said, Some say that thou art John the Baptist: some, Elias, and others, Jeremias, or one of the prophets. He saith unto them, But whom say ye that

I am? And Simon Peter answered and said, Thou are the Christ, the Son of the living God.

Wisdom and insight had come through divine revelation.

And Jesus answered and said unto him, Blessed art thou Simon Bar-jo'na: for flesh and blood hath not revealed it unto thee, but my Father which is in heaven.

And I say also unto thee, Thou art Peter, and upon this rock I will build my church: and the gates of hell shall not prevail against it. (Matthew 16:13, 16–18)

The church was to be built upon the divine revelation of truth and profession of faith Peter had just spoken regarding Jesus.

Remember, Jesus said, "I will build my church."

Please let us not fire the Holy Spirit, the presence of God, and do our own thing! We will have to answer to God if we do.

Concerning Jesus's Glory

When he was transfigured, Jesus showed a preview of his exaltation and the coming kingdom. Three disciples saw his body of glory.

And after six days Jesus taketh Peter, James, and John his brother, and bringeth them up into an high mountain apart, And was transfigured before them: and his face did shine as the sun, and his raiment was white as the light. And, behold, there appeared unto them Moses and Elias talking with him. Then answered Peter, and said unto Jesus, Lord, it is good for us to be here: if thou wilt, let us make here three tabernacles; one for thee, and one for Moses, and one for Elias. While he yet spake, behold, a bright cloud overshadowed them: and behold a voice out of the cloud, which said, This is my beloved son, in whom I am well pleased; hear ye him.

The Presence of God

> And when the disciples heard it, they fell on their face, and were so afraid. And Jesus came and touched them, and said, Arise, and be not afraid. (Matthew 17:1–7)

Has the Lord touched you lately? Don't fool me now!

The Day of Pentecost, the Birthday of the Church

> And when the day of Pentecost was fully come, they were all with one accord in one place.

Casting Lots

The apostles had cast lots, and the lot had fallen upon Matthias. Therefore, Matthias had been numbered with the eleven apostles.

Power from on High

> And suddenly there came a sound from heaven as of a rushing mighty wind, and it filled all the house where they were sitting. And there appeared unto them cloven tongues like as of fire, and it sat upon each of them. And they were all filled with the Holy Ghost, and began to speak with other tongues, as the Spirit gave them utterance. (Acts 2:1–4)

We can clearly see the presence of God at work.
Remember Babel? God confused the language of the people and nations were dispersed to stop evil from spreading.

> Go to, let us go down, and there confound their language, that they may not understand one another's speech.

We see the work of the Trinity again—Father, Son, and Holy Spirit.

The people wanted to build a city and tower whose top reach unto heaven. This tower was not to worship God. But, serve to make a name for them. (Genesis 11:4, 7)

A Reversal

At Pentecost, God brought Jews from many nations together in Jerusalem.

> And there were dwelling at Jerusalem Jews, devout men, out of every nation under heaven. Now when this was noised abroad, the multitude came together, and were confound, because that every man heard them speak in his own language. And they were all amazed and marvelled, saying one to another, Behold, are not all these which speak Galilaeans? And how hear we every man in our own tongue, wherein we were born? And they were all amazed, and were in doubt, saying one to another, What meaning this? Others mocking said, These men are full of new wine.

Peter Preached Christ's Message to Unbelievers

> But Peter, standing up with the eleven, lifted up his voice, and said unto them, Ye men of Judaea, and all ye that dwell at Jerusalem, be this known unto you, and hearken to my words:

> For these are not drunken, as ye suppose, seeing it is but the third hour (9 am) of the day. But this is that which was spoken by the prophet Jo'el; And it shall come to pass in the last days, saith God, I will pour out of my spirit upon all flesh: and your sons and your daughters shall prophesy, and young men shall see visions, and your old men shall dream dreams.

> Therefore let all the house of Israel know assuredly that God hath made that same Jesus, whom ye have crucified both Lord and Christ.

> Now when they heard this, they were pricked in their heart, and said unto Peter and to the rest of the apostles, Men and brethren, what shall we do?

Repentance

> Then Peter said unto them, Repent, and be baptized every one of you in the name of Jesus Christ for the remission of sins, and ye shall receive the gift of the Holy Ghost. (Acts 2:1–8, 12–17, 36–38)

Peter was telling them to change their minds especially concerning Jesus of Nazareth, the Son of God, and to accept him as their Messiah, God, and as Christ, their Lord. Peter's preaching did not fall on deaf ears; some three thousand believers were added to the church that day.

Jesus had given Peter the keys to the kingdom of heaven and thus the authority to open the doors of Christendom (Christian people). Being a Christian is Christlike. Peter had the authority and the weapon of the truth.

Water Baptism

Water baptism is a show of obedience, an outward sign to the world and others that we have made a confession of faith and placed our hope, faith, and belief in Christ.

Some people believe this saying, and some folks do not. That's OK. Remember, we must be saved before we go down into that water. The word of God cleans us!

> Now ye are clean through the word which I have spoken unto you. (John 15:3)

Physical water washes away only dirt, not sin. Several times, my husband, Tommie, has stated to me that one has to be saved before going down into the water to be baptized. "You go down into that water a dry devil, and only comes up a wet devil!" he has often said.

Those are some harsh but true words unless something supernatural happens in that water.

We know God is all powerful, therefore, he is omnipotent.

God knows all things, therefore, he is omniscient.

God can be everywhere therefore, he is omnipresent.

Because of belief and faith in the finished work of the cross, in a twinkling of an eye, God can move and an unbeliever can be saved even while being baptized, amen!

The Holy Spirit baptizes us into the body of Christ. This is a spiritual, not a physical act.

> For by one Spirit are we all baptized into one body, whether we be Jews or Gentiles, whether we be bond or free; and have been all made to drink into one Spirit. (1 Corinthians 12:13)

I will build my church! The words Jesus had spoken to Peter concerning his church had come to pass on the Day of Pentecost, the birthday of the church.

Sometimes, the physical church can be disappointing, lonesome, frustrating, and hurtful. Have you ever been hurt by church folks? It's not a good feeling, right?

Have you ever noticed what we call cliques and tricks in some churches?

If you are not a friend or a yes person in some churches, you may find yourself left out in the cold.

When seeking a church home, keep in mind the holy scriptures and let the Holy Spirit be your guide.

The body of Christ is a group of baptized believers. Are we still in agreement? I am not speaking of water baptism but being baptized into the body of Christ by the Holy Spirit, the presence of God.

Look for saved, Holy Spirit–filled people in the church, that is, church members bearing the fruit of the Spirit.

Some folks may ask, what is saved?
I am glad you asked.

In Search of Salvation

Most of us have read or heard these scriptures.

> Believe on the Lord Jesus Christ and thy shall be saved.

> That if thou shall confess with thy mouth, believe in thy heart that God has raised him from the dead, thou shall be saved. (Romans 10:9)

> For with the heart man believeth unto righteousness, and with the mouth confession is made unto salvation. (Romans 10:10)

> Whosoever shall call upon the name of the Lord, shall be saved. (Romans 10:13)

> So then Faith cometh by hearing, and hearing by the word of God. (Romans 10:17)

Some point out that Paul was addressing Israel in these scriptures, and these scriptures are composed of works. What are your thoughts? We know Israel rejected the Messiah, the Lord Jesus Christ. Did not Israel know? We know Israel must make a confession that Jesus is Lord because of its rejection, amen.

> God has not cast away his people which he foreknew. Wot ye not what the scriptures saith of Elias? How he maketh intercession to God against Israel, saying, Lord, they have killed thy prophets, and digged down thine altars; and I am left alone, and they seek my life. But what saith the answer of God unto him? I have reserved to myself seven thousand men, who have not bowed the knee to the image of Baal.

Even so then at this present time, also there is a remnant according to the election of Grace. (Romans 11:2–5)

Israel's Rejection of Christ

I say then, Have they stumbled that they should fall? God forbid: but rather through their fall salvation is come unto the Gentiles, for to provoke them to jealousy.

Paul, the Apostle to the Gentiles

For I speak to you Gentiles, inasmuch as I am the apostle of the Gentiles, I magnify mine office. (Romans 11:11, 13)

But contrariwise, when they saw that the gospel of the uncircumcision (Gentiles) was committed unto me, as the gospel of the circumcision (Jews) was unto Peter. (Galatians 2:7)

For I would not, brethren, that ye be ignorant of this mystery, lest ye should be wise in your own conceits; that blindness in part is happened to Israel, until the fulness of the Gentiles be come in. And so all Israel shall be saved: as it is written, There shall come out of Sion the Deliverer, and shall turn away ungodliness from Jacob: For this is my covenant unto them, when I shall take away their sins. (Romans 11:25–27)

God is merciful! Jesus has provided grace and mercy for us all. God we praise!

The Israelites lost their favored position with God when they rejected their Messiah, Jesus.

When Jesus returns, Israel will be regathered, judged, restored, and redeemed.

Now, any unsaved person has to believe and by faith accept the finish work of the cross, and then the Holy Spirit, the presence of God, will seal them.

The finished work of the cross is the death, burial, and resurrection of our Lord and Savior Jesus Christ.

If we confess, are baptized in the name of Jesus, tarry for the Holy Spirit, and speak in tongues, some would say that we are working to be saved.

What are your thoughts on that?

The thief on the cross asked Jesus to remember him when he came into his kingdom.

Was this thief baptized? Or did the thief exercise faith?

> And Jesus said unto him, Verily, I say unto thee, To day, shalt thou be with me in Paradise. (Luke 23:43)

There was no tarrying for the Holy Spirit or water baptism done here.

In today's society, can a person be saved like this?

Gospel of Your Salvation

Paul stated,
> In whom ye trusted, after that ye heard the word of truth, the gospel of your salvation, in whom also after that ye believe, ye were sealed with that Holy Spirit of promise. (Ephesians 1:13)

After we have heard and received the gospel, our salvation is secure.

This scripture takes us back to "Whosoever shall call on the name of the Lord shall be saved."

Please do not allow anyone to take away your joy.

The Holy Spirit seals us and baptizes us into the body of Christ. This blessing comes to us because of God's grace and mercy.

No Works Here to Earn Salvation

> For by Grace are you saved through faith, and that not of yourself; it is the gift of God. Not of works, lest any man should boast. (Ephesians 2:8–9)

According to Paul and James, we cannot work to be saved.

James

> Yea, a man may say, Thou hast faith, and I have works:
> shew me thy faith without thy works, and I will shew thee
> my faith by my works. (James 2:18)

James was simply stating that we produce good works, a living, productive trust in Christ, because we are saved. A faith that does not produce good works is a dead faith, no ifs, ands, or buts about it. Good works can be exercised in the church and in our homes, neighborhoods, and in the missionary field.

Remember, works do not earn us salvation.

> But now, O Lord, Thou art our father: we are the clay,
> and thou our potter; and we all are the work of thy hand.
> (Isaiah 64:6–8)

Shall we continue in sin after placing our faith in Christ? God forbid!

Confession of Sin

> If we say that we have no sin, we deceive ourselves, and
> the truth is not in us.

> If we confess our sins, he is faithful and just to forgive us
> our sins, and to cleanse us from all unrighteousness. My
> little children, these things write I unto you, that ye sin
> not, And if any man sin, we have an advocate with the
> Father, Jesus Christ the righteous. (1 John 1:8–9, 2:1)

Scripture calls us to assemble. Again, in the church, look for encouragement, support of the saints, love, fellowship of the Word, scripture-abiding believers, administration of the supper, and love of the Lord.

Please do not entertain a church where you are often condemned by the pastor or members seeking to place you in hell when you do not line up with their agenda.

If you are a child of God, you have the Holy Spirit in you to lead, guide, and direct your path.

Something to remember in the local church: follow a pastor, church members, and leaders as they follow Christ.

The Pastor

The pastor is most likely the chief officer and a servant.

The pastor should be a man with Christian characteristics that please God.

The pastor should be no respecter of persons.

The pastor is to preach the gospel and have
oversight of the work of the church.

The pastor must study, teach, preach, lead, exhort, and reprove knowing that one day, he will have to face God for his actions.

The pastor should be just.

The pastor should be saved.

The pastor should be paid.

The pastor should not look to get rich for preaching God's Word.

Again, in the church, look for Christians bearing the fruit of the Spirit starting with the pastor.

> But the fruit of the spirit is Love, joy, peace, longsuffering, gentleness, goodness, faith, meekness, and temperance: against such there is no law. (Galatians 5:22–23)

The fruit of the Spirit was found in Jesus and must be ever so present in all Christians as well!

CHAPTER 11

❧

HOW CAN THEY PREACH?

Isaiah, who valued the preaching of the Word, was often called the Evangelical Prophet.

> In the year that King Uzziah died, I saw also the Lord sitting upon a throne, high and lifted up, and his train filled the temple. (Isaiah 6:1)

The presence of God filled the place.

> Above it stood the seraphims: each one had six wings; with twain he covered his face, and with twain he covered his feet, and with twain he did fly. And one cried unto another, and said, Holy, holy, holy, is the Lord of hosts: the whole earth is full of his glory. And the post of the door moved at the voice of him that cried, and the house was filled with smoke.

The power of God caused the foundation to move.

Isaiah Confessed and Repented

> Then said I, Woe is me! for I am undone; because I am a man of unclean lips, and I dwell in the midst of a people

of unclean lips: for mines eyes have seen the King, The Lord of Hosts.

Are you willing to concur with Isaiah?

The Cleansing Process

Then flew one of the Seraphims unto me, having a live coal in his hand, which he had talen with the tongs from off the the altar. And he laid it upon my mouth, and said, Lo, this hath touched thy lips; and thine iniquity is taken away, and thy sin purged.

Isaiah communed with the Lord and received his commission.

Also I heard the voice of the Lord, saying, Whom shall I send, and who will go for us? Then, said I, Here am I; send me. Send me to do your will Lord, especially to preach your word. A willing heart indeed is required!

We also see the Trinity at work.

And he said, Go, and tell this people, Hear ye indeed, but understand not; and see ye indeed, but perceive not. (Isaiah 6:1–9)

We know how God inspired Isaiah to write Isaiah 53.

Why Did Jesus Suffer and Die?

Taking Heed after Hearing the Message of the Gospel
A sinner may ask, "What must I do to be saved?"
What is God's simple plan of salvation? What would you tell a sinner?

For God so loved the world that he gave his only begotten son, that whosoever believeth in him should not perish, but have everlasting life. (John 3:16)

You should advise a sinner,

> If thou shall confess with thy mouth the Lord Jesus, and shalt believe in thine heart that God hath raised him from the dead, thou shalt be saved. For with the heart man believeth unto righteousness; and the mouth confession is made unto salvation. For the scripture saith, whosoever believeth on him shall not be ashamed. For there is no difference between the Jew and the Greek: for the same Lord over all is rich unto all that call upon him. For whosoever shall call upon the name of the lord shall be saved. How then shall they call on him in whom they have not believed? and how shall they believe in him of whom they have not heard? and how shall they hear without a preacher? And how shall they preach, except they be sent? as it is written, How beautiful are the feet of them that preach the gospel of peace, and bring glad tidings of good things. (Romans 10:9–15)

In Ephesians 1:13, we read,

> In whom ye also trusted, after that ye heard the word of truth, the gospel of your salvation: In whom also after that ye believed, ye were sealed with that Holy Spirit of promise.

Our salvation is sealed; we are guaranteed of security of our salvation, and no one can take it away from us.

But what should they preach and teach? The gospel of peace, good tiding, and of course, salvation.

The Great Commission—The Missionary Task of the Church

> And Jesus came and spake unto them, saying, all power is geven unto me in heaven and in earth, Go ye therefore, and teach all nations, baptizing them in the name of the father, and of the Son, and of the Holy Ghost. Go and make disciples of all nations! Teaching them to observe all things whatsoever I have command you: and, lo, I

am with you always, even unto the end of the world. (Matthew 28:18–20)

Does this Great Commission apply to the body of Christ as well, or was it just for the disciples?

The death, burial, and resurrection of our Lord and Savior Jesus Christ are to be preached and taught. As Christians, members of the body of Christ, in these times of trouble, what are we supposed to be doing? As Christians, are we exercising faith? Are we encouraging others? Are we displaying peace, grace, and mercy to others? Or are we showing our doubt in these times of trouble?

Remember Doubting Thomas? There is no room for doubt on this Christian journey!

> But Thomas, one of the twelve, called Didymus, was not with them when Jesus came. The other disciples therefore said unto him, We have seen the Lord, But he said unto them, Except I shall see in his hands the print of the nails, and put my finger into the print of the nails, and thrust my hand into his side, I will not believe.

Jesus in Their Midst

> And after eight days again his disciples were within, and Thomas with them: then came Jesus, the doors being shut, and stood in the midst, and said, Peace be unto you. Then said he to Thomas, Reach hither thy finger, and behold my hands; and reach hither thy hand, thrust it into my side: and be not faithless, but believing. And Thomas answered and said unto him, My Lord and my God. Jesus saith unto him, Thomas, because thou hast seen me, thou has believed: Blessed are they that have not seen, and yet have believed. (John 20:24–29)

Brothers and sisters in the faith, that's us!

Men and women cannot preach or teach the gospel and other scriptures effectively if they themselves do not believe the gospel.

God is still alive and well.

God—the Holy Spirit, dwells in me. He leads, guides, and directs my path. But I have to be a willing participator.

Let's pay attention to the men and women called by God, not by man or by themselves for all the wrong reasons.

Too often, we find pastors called by man rather than God. If their fathers were pastors, it is only fitting and proper that they become pastors; that's the thinking of many churches. What does God have to say about that? If God did the calling, there is no problem with the format.

Israel Was Allowed to Have Kings

Despite Samuel's warning, the Israelites demanded a king.

> Nevertheless the people refused to obey the voice of Samuel; and they said, Nay, but we will have a king over us; That we may be like other nations; and that our king may judge us, and go out before us, and fight our battles. (1 Samuel 8:19–20)

Samuel had grown old. He had made his sons judges over Israel. That was a big mistake.

> Samuel's sons walked not in his ways, they turned aside after lucre, and took bribes, and perverted judgments.

Samuel prayed to God, and the Lord revealed to Samuel that kings would bring about problems for the people. Samuel made known the revelations below to the people but to no avail.

1. The king would draft their young into his army.
2. The king would tax their flocks and crops.
3. The king would take their fields and vineyards.
4. The king would take the tenth and give it to his officers.
5. The king would take their menservants and maidservants and their asses and put them to work.

> And the Lord said unto Samuel, harken unto the voice of
> the people in all that they say unto thee; for they have not
> rejected thee, but they have rejected me, that I should not
> reign over them. (1 Samuel 8:7, 11, 13–16)

God allowed the children of Israel to have their first king, a handsome
man, King Saul; Bible scholars know the conclusion of that era. Later, God
repented having allowed King Saul to have been king over Israel.

David—God's Choice

> And he (Samuel) went, and brought him in. Now he
> was ruddy, and withal of a beautiful countenance, and
> goodly to look to. And the Lord said, arise, anoint him:
> For this is he. Then Samuel took the horn of oil, and
> anointed him in the midst of his brethren: and the spirit
> of the Lord (Presence of God) came upon David from that
> day forward. So Samuel rose up, and went to Ramah. (1
> Samuel 16:12–13)

In many instances, Holy Spirit–filled preachers are left out, overlooked,
or put on the back burner because they have not found favor with the
right people including leaders, moderators, pastors, deacons, trustees, and
members.

As in the days of King Saul, God is still watching, and he is not pleased
when this happen.

The son of Jesse, David, a man after God's own heart, became Israel's
second king. David's reign pleased God. He was God's choice for service.

> David was thirty years old when he began to reign, and he
> reigned forty years. In Hebron he reigned over Judah seven
> years and six months: And in Jerusalem, he reigned thirty
> and three years over all Israel and Judah. (2 Samuel 5:4–5)

CHAPTER 12

❧

PAUL, THE APOSTLE TO THE GENTILES, AND STEPHEN, THE FIRST MARTYR

Paul spoke to King Agrippa.

> At midday, O King, I saw in the way a light from heaven, above the brightness of the sun, shining round about me, and them which journeyed with me. And when we were all fallen to the earth, I heard a voice speaking unto me, and saying in the Hebrew tongue, Saul, Saul, why persecutest thou me? it is hard for thee to kick against the pricks.

Jesus Stops Saul

Your arms are too short to box with God, Saul! Saul was born in Tarsus of Cilicia. He was a Jew, a Pharisee, and a Roman citizen.

He was a teacher of the law. He studied under Gamaliel, a Jewish scholar, in Jerusalem. And Saul persecuted the saints. He was on his way to Damascus to capture Christians and bring them to Jerusalem to be punished, but Jesus intervened.

When Jesus Speaks

And I said, Who art thou, Lord? and he said, I am Jesus whom thou persecutest. But rise, and stand upon thy feet: for I have appeared unto thee for this purpose; to make thee a minister and a witness both of these things which thou hast seen, and of those things in the which I will appear unto thee; Delivering thee from the people, and from the Gentiles unto whom now I send thee. To open their eyes, and to turn them from darkness to light, and from the power of Satan unto God, that they may receive forgiveness of sins, and inheritance among them which are sanctified by faith that is in me.

Was Paul Obedient?

Whereupon, O King Agrippa, I was not disobedient unto the heavenly vision: But shewed first unto them of Damascus, and at Jerusalem, and throughout all the coasts of Judaea, and then to the Gentiles, that they should repent and turn to God, and do works meet for repentance. For these causes the Jews caught me in the temple, and went about to kill me.

The Lord Helped Paul

Having therefore obtained help from God, I continue unto this day, witnessing both to small and great, saying none other things than those which the prophets and Moses did say should come. That Christ should suffer, and that he should be the first that should rise from the dead, and should shew light unto the people, and to the Gentiles. And as he thus spake for himself, Festus (a Roman could not understand) said with a loud voice, Paul, thou art beside thyself; much learning doth make thee mad.

Festus was a Roman; he could not comprehend Paul's statements.

But he said, I am not mad, most noble Festus; but speak forth the words of truth and soberness. For the King knoweth of these things, before whom also I speak freely: For I am persuaded that none of these things are hidden from him; for this thing was not done in a corner. King Agrippa, believest thou the prophets? I know that thou believest.

The King Had His Chance to Be Saved

Then Agrippa, said unto Paul, Almost thou persusdest me to be a Christian. (Acts 26:13–28)

Almost, King Agrippa? Remember, King Agrippa was a Jew. Paul felt the king would understand his point.

The Mystery

For this cause I paul, the prisoner of Jesus Christ for you Gentiles. If ye have heard of the dispensation of the grace of God which is given to you-ward: How that by revelation he made known unto me the mystery; (as I wrote afore in few words, Whereby, when ye read, ye may understand my knowledge in the mystery of Christ) Which in other ages was not made known unto the sons of men, as it is now revealed unto his holy apostles and prophets by the Spirit.

God Loves Us All—Jews and Gentiles Are Equal Heirs

That the Gentiles should be fellow heirs, and of the same body, and partakers of his promise in Christ by the gospel. Whereof I was made a minister, according to the gift of the grace of God given unto me by the effectual working of his power. Unto me, who am less than the least of all saints, is this grace given, that I should preach among the Gentiles the unsearchable riches of Christ; And to make all men see what is the fellowship of the mystery, which from the beginning of the world hath been HID in God, who created all things by Jesus Christ. (Ephesians 3:1--9)

Salvation made available to us Gentiles! Thank you, Jesus. The Jews' Rejection

I say then, have they stumbled that they should fall? God forbid: but rather through their fall, salvation is come unto the Gentiles, for to provoke them to jealousy. Now if the fall of them be the riches of the world, and the diminishing of them the riches of the Gentiles; how much more their fulness? For I speak to you Gentiles, inasmuch as I am the Apostle of the Gentiles, I magnify mine office. (Romans 11:11–13)

When Israel rejected Christ, it lost its favored position before the Almighty and the Gentiles received the gospel.

God's plan is that the Jews received the gospel, repent, and be regathered, judged, and restored.

Stephen

No one person can do it all; we need each other. The early church was advised to look among themselves for seven men of honest report who were full of the Holy Spirit and wisdom to become deacons.

A murmuring of the Greeks arose against the Hebrews because they felt their widows were being neglected in the daily ministration.

The disciples wanted to continue to give themselves to the ministry of the Word.

(Revisit Acts 6:1–4.)

And the saying pleased the whole multitude: and they chose Stephen, a man full of faith and of the Holy Ghost, and Philip, and Proch'orus, and Nica'nor, and Ti'mon, and Par'menas, and Nicolas a proselyte of Antioch.

A proselyte is a person who has changed from one religion or political party to another.

> Whom they set before the apostles: and when they had prayed, they laid hands on them. (Acts 6:1, 3–6)

The laying on of hands was a sign of appointment to the service prayed for.

Pastors, Deacons, and Other Ministers Are Servants

> Likewise must the deacons be grave, not doubletongued, not given to much wine, not greedy of fithy lucre; Holding the mystery of the faith in a pure conscience. And let these also first be proved then let them use the office of a deacon, being found blameless.

Deacons' Wives

> Even so must their wives be grave, not slanderers, sober faithful in all things. Let the deacons be the husbands of one wife, ruling their children and their own houses well. (1 Timothy 3:8–12)

Stephen—A Man Filled with the Holy Spirit

> And Stephen, full of faith and power, did great wonders and miracles among the people.

It's not strange that Satan's workers and unbelieving Jews were still on the scene.

> And they were not able to resist the wisdom and spirit by which he spake. Then they suborned (secretly instigated) men, which said, We have heard him speak blasphemous words against Moses, and against God. And they stirred

up the people, and the elders, and the scribes, and came upon him, and caught him, and brought him to the council.

Stephen on Trial

The council was the Sanhedrin, the supreme court for the Jews.

And they set up false witnesses, which said, This man ceaseth not to speak blasphemous words against this holy place, and the law.

Sounds familiar, right?

Stephen's enemies came from the synagogue. A number of Hebrews were contaminated with ethnic prejudice.

For we have heard him say, that this Jesus of Nazareth shall destroy this place, and shall change the customs which Moses delivered to us.

And all that sat in the council, looking stedfastly on him, saw his face as it had been the face of an angel.

Stephen's angelic face should have been enough to cause them to stop their evildoing.

Beware of the sealed consciences of men! These people have no remorse for what they do or say that hurts others. They have no reverence for God or the mission of believers to spread His Word. Stephen charged the men.

Ye stiffnecked and uncircumcised in heart and ears, ye do always resist the Holy Ghost: as your Fathers did, so do ye. Which of the prophets have not your fathers persecuted? and they have slain them which shewed before of the coming of the just one; whom ye have been now the betrayer and murderers. Who have received the law by the disposition of angels, and have not kept it. When they heard these things, they were cut to the heart, and they gnashed on him with their teeth.

The unbelieving Jews became very angry with Stephen because of the truth he had spoken.

But he, being full of the Holy Ghost, looked up stedfastly into heaven, and saw the "glory of God" and Jesus standing on the right hand of God.

Stephen Saw Jesus

And said, Behold, I see the heavens opened, and the Son of Man standing on the right hand of God. Then they cried out with a loud voice, and stopped their ears, and ran upon him with one accord.

They Murdered Stephen

And cast him out of the city, and stoned him: and the witnesses laid down their clothes at a young man's feet, whose name was Saul.

Now, It's On You, Saul!

And they stoned Stephen, calling upon God, saying Lord Jesus, receive my spirit. And he kneeled down, and cried with a loud voice, Lord, lay not this sin to their charge. And when he had said this, he fell asleep. (Acts 6:8, 10–15, 7:51–60)

Remember the words of our Savior.

Father forgive them; for they know not what they do. And they parted his raiment, and cast lots. (Luke 23:34)

The Christians scattered fearing for their lives and especially Saul, who had been present when conflicts with the council and Stephen arose.

Saul set out to destroy as many Christians as he could. Many Christians fled to Damascus to escape the persecution of Saul after Stephen's death.

But God

After Paul's conversion, Paul preached and taught the Word to the Gentiles. God has not changed. He still wants Holy Spirit–filled pastors, teachers, deacons, and others leaders to edify the body.

We should work not to consume ourselves in raising and always begging God's people for money for our own glory.

What about dwelling in the Spirit, abiding in the Word, and recruiting souls for Christ?

Paul said,

This is a true saying, If a man desire the office of a bishop, he desireth a good work. A bishop then must be blameless, the husband of one wife, vigilant, sober, of good behavior, given to hospitality, apt to teach. Not given to wine, no striker, not greedy of filthy lucre but patient, not a brawer, not covetous. One that ruleth well his own house, having his children in subjection with all gravity. (1 Timothy 3:1–4)

The apostle Paul said yes to God's calling and was obedient to the end. And there are differences of administrations but the same Lord.

Are you aware of your ministry?

Are you exercising it?

And God has set some in the church, first apostles, secondarily, prophets, thirdly, teachers, after that miracles, then gifts of healings, helpers, governments, diversities of tongues. (1 Corinthians 12:5, 28)

We can clearly see the presence of God in the callings of these different administrations for the edification of the church.

CHAPTER 13

CAUGHT UP—THE RAPTURE

Most of us are familiar with the phrase *the Rapture*. The holy scriptures use the words *caught up* for the Rapture.

Many, and especially the faithful, have wondered what happens after death. At many funerals, we have often been reassured that we will see our loved ones again and that they are only sleeping. Our great hope and faith rest in the belief that Jesus is coming back for us.

We are often comforted remembering the words of our Lord and Savior, Jesus Christ;

> Let not your heart be troubled: ye believe in God, believe also in me. In my Father's house are many mansions: if it were not so, I would have told you. I go to prepare a place for you. And if I go and prepare a place for you, I will come again, and receive you unto myself; that where I am, there ye may be also. And whither I go ye know, and the way ye know. Thomas saith unto him, Lord, we know not whither thou goest; and how can we know the way? Jesus saith unto him, I am the way, the truth, and the life: no man cometh unto the Father, but by me. (John 14:1–6)

We have familiarized ourselves with the phrase *absent from the body present with the Lord.*

When people die, we are happy to know that their spirits return to God.

While We Are Alive

Therefore we are always confident, knowing that, whilst we are at home in the body, we are absent from the Lord. (For we walk by faith, not by sight) We are confident, I say, and willing rather to be absent from the body, and to be present with the Lord.

Be Content if You Belong to Christ

Wherefore we labour, that, whether present or absent, we may be accept of him. (2 Corinthians 5:6–9)

When Jesus Comes for His Church

For the Lord himself shall descend from heaven with a shout, and with the voice of the archangel, and with the trump of God: and the dead in Christ shall rise first.

Those who died after accepting Christ as their Savior will rise first when Christ comes for his church, the body of Christ.

Then we which are alive and remain shall be Caugh Up together with them in the clouds to meet the Lord in the air: and so shall we ever be with the Lord. Wherefore comfort one another with these words. (1 Thessalonians 4:16–18)

Remember, Jesus will appear in the air, not on earth.

We Will Be Changed

Behold, I shew you a mystery; We shall not all sleep, but we shall all be changed, In a moment, in the twinkling

of an eye, at the last trump: for the trumpet shall sound,
and the dead shall be raised incorruptible, and we shall
be changed.

We know flesh and blood cannot inherit the kingdom of God, right?

For this corruptible must put on incorruption, and this
mortal must put on immortality.

Corruptible refers to the ones who have died. Mortals refers to those
who are living.

So, when this corruptible shall have put on incorruptible,
and this mortal shall have put on immortality, then shall
be brought to pass the saying that is written, Death is
swallowed up in victory.

Death

O death, where is thy sting? O grave, where is thy victory?
The sting of death is sin; and the strength of sin is the law.
(1 Corinthians 15:51–55)

Sin brought about death. Remember Adam and Eve in the garden?

The strength of sin is the Law. The Law stirs up sin. But
thanks be to God, which giveth us the victory through
our Lord Jesus Christ. (1 Corinthians 15:57)

Death gained authority over us because of sin. Jesus won that battle
for us! Our long-awaited Savior, Jesus, will return and take the body of
Christ, the saved believers, back with him to heaven.

Therefore, my belief lies in the premillennial theory, which says the
church, the body of Christ, will be caught up and return with Jesus Christ
to set up the millennial kingdom.

The Rapture Will Happen Prior to the Tribulation

The word *tribulation* refers to great misery or trouble for the unbelievers left after the Rapture.

How can we forget the tribulations, storms, or troubles of Job, a righteous man?

And then there was Jonah, who came to himself in the belly of a whale. Remember the troubles of the Israelites?

> God told Moses to forsake not to remind the children of Israel, and to tell their children of their ordeal, and how their ancestors were delivered from Egypt by the hands of a mighty God.

The children of Israel suffered great tribulation by the hands of their taskmasters, the Egyptians.

We shall never forget the coronavirus pandemic, which has affected unbelievers and believers alike.

Word to the wise: Hold onto the vehicle you're riding in. That vehicle should be Jesus Christ our Lord!

During the covid pandemic, many suffered shortages of food, water, money, transportation, and much more. Churchgoers couldn't meet in church, and many had to quarantine after they caught the virus. Many suffered from the virus, and so many died as a result of it.

This is a storm to remember, but God is still in control, and he has the last word on our survival and well-being.

This pandemic storm can in no way be compared to the troubles entailed during the Great Tribulation for those left after the Rapture.

Doing the Tribulation, we find the rise of the Antichrist, the mark of the beast, world religion, torment, famine, death ... The list goes on ...

> For many deceivers are entered into the world, who confess not that Jesus Christ is come in the flesh. This is a deceiver and an antichrist. (2 John 7)

Revelation talks more about this Antichrist and the beast, the false prophet, and the number associated with the Antichrist.

> Here is wisdom, Let him that hath understanding count the number of the beast: for it is the number of a man; and his number is Six hundred threescore and six. (Revelation 13:18)

The dispensation of grace will be over. The Tribulation will last seven years. Some unbelievers may obtain salvation during the Tribulation but will suffer great at the hands of the Antichrist and his workers. During the first three and a half years of the Tribulation, many will be deceived by the Antichrist. The last three and a half years is called the Great Tribulation.

The Millennium period comes after the Tribulation; this is a time when believers will be awarded with the presence of Jesus.

This will be a peaceful time because Satan will be bound for a thousand years.

> And I saw an angel come down from heaven having the key of the bottomless pit and a great chain in his hand. And he laid hold on the dragon, that old serpent, which is the Devil, and Satan, and bound him a thousand years. And cast him into the bottomless pit, and shut him up, and set a seal upon him, that he should deceive the nations no more, till the thousand years should be fulfilled: and after that he must be loosed a little season. (Revelation 20:1–3)

Martyrs of the Great Tribulation

John wrote,

> And I saw thrones, and they sat upon them, and judgment was given unto them: and I saw the souls of them that were beheaded for the witness of Jesus, and for the word of God, and which had not worshipped the beast, neither his image, neither had received his mark upon their their foreheads, or in their hands; and they lived and reigned with Christ a thousand years. (Revelation 20:4)

Satan Loosed Again—His Final Attempt to Overthrow Christ

> And when the thousand years are expired, Satan shall be
> loosed out of his prison, And shall go out to deceive the
> nations which are in the four quarters of the earth, Gog
> and Ma'gog, (world wide enemies of Jesus) to gather them
> together to battle: the number of whom is as the sand of
> the sea. And they went up on the breadth of the earth, and
> compassed the camp of the saints about, and the beloved
> city: and fire came down from God out of heaven, and
> devoured them. (Revelation 20:7–9)

We shall read about the "doom" of Satan in chapter 14.
Keep reading!

CHAPTER 14

⚬᪻⚬

THE LAKE OF FIRE

John the Revelator stated that he was in the Spirit, in the presence of God, on the Lord's Day.

> I John, who also am your brother, and companion in tribulation, and in the kingdom and patience of Jesus Christ, was in the isle that is called Patmos, for the word of God: and for the testimony of Jesus Christ. I was in the Spirit on the Lord's day, and heard behind me a great voice, as a trumpet, Saying, I am Alpha and Omega, the first and the last: and, What thou seest, write in a book, and send it unto the seven churches which are in Asia; unto Eph'esus, and unto Smyrna, and unto Per'gamos, and unto 'Thyati'ra, and unto Sardis, and unto Philadelphia, and unto Laodice'a. (Revelation 1:9–11)

Lord knows I am not John or an apostle. The Bible has already been written by Spirit-filled and inspired men of God. But I am a child of God, a follower of Christ, and one who waits for the return of our Lord and Savior Jesus Christ for his church.

It hard to tell whether I was dreaming or seeing a vision when these events involving the lake of fire were revealed to me by God.

My awareness found me in the midst of the lake of fire being accompanied by two angels who were holding my arms. The angels were dressed in white. I was unable to look upon their faces, but I had no desire to do so. I just trusted that they were from God and would protect me. The angels affirmed my trust by advising me not to be afraid.

They wanted to show me something. Somehow, we ended up standing on a long, solid, white, and strong platform extending out into the lake of fire, but I did not feel the heat.

One angel told me to look up, down, and all around. All I saw everywhere were red and orange flames. When I began to feel frightened, the angels reassured me that I was in no danger.

A long, deep, high burning pit of fire was all I could see. There was no way out!

My last command from the angels was to look behind me. I turned and saw three figures. I saw what appeared to be my dear mama dressed in white, an angel, and a child of about four or five holding their hands.

Far behind Mama, the child, and the angel were more orange and red flames as far as the eyes could see, but Mama, the child, and the angel were safe as they stood on a strong, solid, white platform that was a great distance from the flames.

The dream or vision ended. I came to the conclusion that there was no exit from the lake of fire.

The Devil's and the False Prophet's Futures

> And the devil that deceived them was cast into the Lake of Fire and brimstone, where the beast and the false prophet are, and shall be tormented day and night for ever and ever.

The Great White Throne

> And I saw a great white throne, and him that sat on it, from whose face the earth and the heaven fled away; and there was found no place for them.

The Judgment of the Lost

> And I saw the dead small and great, stand before God, and the books were opened: and another book was opened, which is the book of life: and the dead were judged out of those things which were written in the books, according to their works. And the sea gave up the dead which was in it; and death and hell delivered up the dead which was in them: and they were judged every man according to their works. This is the judgment of the unbelieving dead at the end of the Millennium; they will be judged based on their works. During their lives, they had had the opportunity of accepting Christ as Savior, but they had rejected him. And death and hell were cast into the Lake of Fire. This is the second death. And whosoever was not found written in the Book of Life was cast into The Lake of Fire. (Revelation 20:10–15)

Rest assured that I have caught a glimpse of the lake of fire and do not want anyone—family, friends, enemies, haters of God, or me—to be cast into it.

Seek and ye shall find. When God knocks on the door of your heart, open it and let him in.

The Eternal State—A New Heaven and a New Earth in God's Presence for the Saints

> And I saw a new heaven and a new earth: for the first heaven and the first earth were passed away; and there was no more sea.

The present creation we now enjoy will be destroyed and cleansed from the effects of sin, which had its beginning in the garden with Adam and Eve.

The devil has been cast into the late of fire.

> And I John saw the holy city, New Jerusalem, coming down from God out of heaven, prepared as a bride adorned for her husband.

This New Jerusalem is the dwelling place of the saints.

> And I heard a great voice out of heaven saying, behold, the tabernacle of God is with men, and he will dwell with them, and they shall be his people, and God himself shall be with them, and be their God.

Living in the Presence of God Forever—Hallelujah!

> And God shall wipe away all tears from their eyes; and there shall be no more death, neither sorrow, nor crying, neither shall there be any more pain: For the former things are passed away. And he that sat upon the throne said, Behold, I make all things new. And he said unto me, Write: for these words are true and faithful. And he said unto me, It is done. I am Alpha and Omega, the beginning and the end. I will give unto him that is athirst of the fountain of the water of life freely. He that overcometh shall inherit all things; and I will be his God, and he shall be my son.

Hang in there, saints! The Lord has many good rewards for us.

> But the fearful, and unbelieving, and the abominable, and murderers, and whoremongers, and sorcerers, and idolaters, and all liars, shall have their part in the lake which burneth with fire and brimstone: Which is the second death. (Revelation 21:1–8)

Creation and humankind now serve the purpose God had in mind from the beginning, in the garden with Adam and Eve.

Let everything that has breath say, "Praise the Lord!"

CHAPTER 15

◈

THINK ON THESE THINGS

For what is a man profited, if he gains the whole world, and lose his own soul? or what shall a man give in exchange for his soul? (Matthew 16:26)

King Solomon

Solomon, the son of David, a preacher, a great king of Israel at one time, a man known for his wisdom, tried a variety of ways to find happiness and satisfaction apart from God. God must be active in our lives. He is true happiness for those who believe.

What about money or things? They can bring some type of happiness, right?

Solomon possessed great wealth. He had seven hundred wives and three hundred concubines and was a man of wisdom. There is nothing wrong with wealth or wisdom.

Scripture teaches us that if we lack wisdom, we should ask God for it. But having more than one wife is against all that the scriptures teach us.

These things still did not bring King Solomon true happiness. This great man of wisdom wrote,

> Remember now thy Creator in the days of thy youth,
> while the evil days come not, nor the years draw nigh,
> when thou shall say, I have no pleasure in them; While

the sun, or the light, or the moon, or the stars, be not darkened, nor the clouds return after the rain.

Remember God before the storm comes.

Growing Old

In the day when the keepers of the house shall tremble, and the strong men shall bow themselves, and the grinders cease because they are few, and those that look out of the windows be darkened, remember God before your legs become weak and your teeth are few.

> And the doors shall be shut in the streets, when the sound of the grinding is low, and he shall rise up at the voice of the bird, and all the daughters of music shall be brought low.

Remember God before you become hard of hearing.

> Also when they shall be afraid of that which is high, and the almond tree shall flourish, and the grasshopper shall be a burden, and desire shall fail: because man goeth to his long home, and the mourners go about the streets.

Remember God before old age sets in and you have become afraid of falling, your hair is gray, your limbs are impaired, and death is in the near future.

> Or ever the silver cord be loosed, or the golden bowl be broken, or the pitcher be broken at the fountain, or the wheel broken at the cistern.

Remember God before you lose life support.

> Then shall the dust return to the earth as it was: and the spirit shall return unto God who gave it.

After death, man's body returns to dust. The spirit returns to God, who gave it. Vanity of vanities, saith the preacher, all is vanity.

Solomon's Life Lesson

Let us hear the conclusion of the whole matter.

> Fear God, and keep his commandments: For this is the whole duty of man. For God shall bring every work into judgment, with every secret thing, whether it be good or whether it be evil. (Ecclesiastes 12:1–8, 13–14)

Life is empty if we just live for the day without God. As sure as we live, one day we will die if we are not caught up in the Rapture. Therefore, it is important to remember the Lord while we have time.

Love

> Jesus said unto him, Thou shalt love the Lord thy God with all thy heart, and with all thy soul, and with all thy mind. This is the first and great commandment. And the second is like unto it, Thou shalt love thy neighbor as thyself. (Matthew 22:37–39)

You Are a Liar, and the Truth Is Not in You

> If a man say, I love God, and hateth his brother, he is a liar: for he that loveth not his brother whom he hath seen, how can he love God whom he hath not seen? (1 John 4:20)

> You want to walk in darkness, hate your brother! (1 John 2:9)

Are You A Murderer?

> Whosoever hateth his brother is a murderer: and ye
> know that no murderer hath eternal life abiding in him.
> (1 John 3:15)

Why Should We Love Each Other?

> Hereby perceive we the love of God, because he laid down
> his life for us: and we ought to lay down our lives for our
> brethren. And this is his commandment, That we should
> believe on the name of his Son Jesus Christ, and Love one
> another, as he gave us commandment. (1 John 3:16, 23)

> Beloved, let us love one another: for love is of God; and
> every one that loveth is born of God, and knoweth God.
> He that loveth not knoweth not God; for God is Love.
> We love him because he first loved us. (1 John 4:7–8, 19)

> And now abideth Faith, Hope, Charity, these three; but
> the greatest of these is Charity. (1 Corinthians 13:13)

Love expressed and showed God's attributes. A show of love was indeed
displayed by most citizens of the United States during the coronavirus
pandemic. For the most part, our government provided stimulus checks
to many, and celebrities donated large sums of money to help the needy,
and donations of food went to the needy as well.

The citizens the Hoosier State, Indiana, showed their love during the
pandemic by helping many others. Words cannot express the warmth I
felt as I witnessed their gifts of love, money, support, and services to fellow
Hoosiers. The hungry were fed. The homeless were housed. The lonely
and the sick were comforted.

God Knows

> Lord, when did I do these things? When you have done
> it to the least!

Heavenly Father, we come in the name of Jesus. We give you all the honor, praise, and glory!

We love you, Lord, because you first loved us. Lord, allow us to continue to walk in love with each other and treat each other as we wish to be treated.

Thank you for being our prime example of love.

Thank you for being our Provider.

Thank you for being our Comforter.

Thank you for your grace and mercy.

And thank you for salvation.

Thank you for all our first responders, essential workers, doctors, nurses, and other health care staff, law enforcements officers, firefighters, teachers, grocery store workers, transportation staff of various networks, our media, television personalities, election staff and workers, utility workers ... The list goes on ...

Thank you, Lord, for our families, friends, neighbors, pastors, and other brothers and sisters in the faith.

Thank you, Lord, for our leaders who have respect and a reverence for you and who love your people, our church, and our country.

Heavenly Father, please bless the new leader of this great country, President Joe Biden, and the first woman of color and first female vice president, Kamala Harris.

Lord, if we left anyone out, you know who they are and what they brought to the table. Lord Jesus, continue to make the crooked roads straight in our lives and country. Open blind eyes that unbelievers may see and realize that you are the one true God of heaven and earth.

We ask that you calm the storm of this coronavirus and let peace be still in our hearts and minds and in the streets of our fair cities.

Dear Lord, continue to allow your presence to be exercised in our lives, and continue to bless these United States of America and the entire world.

Now Lord, remember all those in the household of faith, in Jesus's name, amen.

ABOUT THE AUTHOR

Betty Ingram Green, a former board of Christian education director for her church, Sunday school superintendent and teacher, and a mentor for young women and girls, a retired substitute teacher and businesswoman, and a writer of poetry and religious plays is an all-around person.

Betty is also the author of the book Bett: The Long Journey, which received a five-star rating. The book, published in 2015, details the author's life growing up in the Deep South during the fifties, sixties, and seventies.

The Presence of God details the religious aspects of the author, her strong beliefs, and her faith in standing on the blessed promises of God.

The book compels readers when searching for a church home in this dispensation of grace to search diligently for the presence of God in everything especially in the physical church's administration of spiritual gifts.

Never fail to exercise the spirit of discernment!